Writing for the GED® Test

4

Practice Prompts for Extended Response and Short Answers

New Readers Press
ProLiteracy's publishing division

Writing for the GED® Test
Practice Prompts for Extended Response and Short Answers
ISBN 978-1-56420-866-8

New Readers Press
ProLiteracy's Publishing Division
104 Marcellus Street, Syracuse, New York 13204
www.newreaderspress.com

Printed in the United States of America
10 9 8 7 6

Proceeds from the sale of New Readers Press materials support professional development, training, and technical assistance programs of ProLiteracy that benefit local literacy programs in the U.S. and around the globe.

Contributing Editor: Steven Schmidt
Assistant Production Editor: Debbie Liehs
Editorial Director: Terrie Lipke
Technology Specialist: Maryellen Casey
Designer: Carolyn Wallace

Contents

REASONING THROUGH LANGUAGE ARTS EXTENDED RESPONSE

The GED® Reasoning Through Language Arts (RLA) Test includes one extended response prompt. You will be asked to read one or more passages and then write about them. On the RLA test, the passages will be arguments. The prompt will ask you to analyze the arguments and then determine which argument is stronger. You will need to cite relevant and specific evidence from the source passages to support your response. Review the scoring rubric on page 108 to see how your response will be scored.

To prepare for the test, keep track of how long it takes you to write your responses. You will have 45 minutes to complete the RLA extended response.

RLA—45 minutes total

1. Read and analyze: 15 minutes

2. Plan and write: 25 minutes

3. Check and revise: 5 minutes

After you finish writing a response, review the scoring rubric. In the Answers and Exemplars that start on page 109, you will find notes about what a good response might include.

Here are some tips for how to score higher on the extended response:

- Write essays that are 4-7 paragraphs and 300-500 words long.
- Paraphrase evidence rather than quoting directly from the source.
- Focus on fully developing two or three main ideas with supporting evidence.
- Write responses based on information in the prompts, not on personal opinion.

The GED test is given on the computer. To practice the RLA extended response on the computer, go to **writing4.newreaderspress.com**. You can read and respond to a practice prompt that looks similar to the one on the GED test. A clock on the screen keeps track of your time. There is also a practice section where you can type your responses to the prompts in this book. When you finish typing a response, you can send it to your teacher. Then your teacher can grade your response.

1: Tattoos

Tattoos: The Ultimate in Expression

By Ron Johnson

Once only seen on sailors, prisoners, and rebels, tattoos are now everywhere. According to the U.S. Food and Drug Administration, about 45 million Americans have tattoos, and there are now over 4,000 tattoo studios across the country. As a tattoo artist, I can tell you there are so many great reasons to get a tattoo!

Tattoos are the ultimate form of expressing yourself. They are a wonderful way to announce to the world who you really are. Tattoos can show your individual personality or connection with a certain group. With a tattoo on board, you will never meet a stranger. Tattoos are natural conversation starters, giving the wearers a great opportunity to share the meaning behind their artwork.

Tattoos are also a great method for commemorating a person or an event. What better way to show your love to others than having their names tattooed on your body? Many people get tattoos to signify an important event in their life like reaching a certain age, getting married, or beating cancer. A tattoo to honor someone's memory means you will always carry that person with you wherever you go.

If you think a tattoo will hold you back in the workplace, you are wrong. John Challenger, the CEO of a consulting firm, says that the majority of employers look more at prospective employees' skills versus their appearance. Challenger says, "Even in this tight job market, most companies aren't going to view tattoos too harshly. Companies have a vested interest in hiring the most qualified candidate."

Unlike the back-alley operators of days past, today's tattoo artists run safe and clean operations. Most are highly trained artists with years of experience. For a small amount of money, they can make your body a beautiful work of art while giving you a unique experience you will never forget!

Think Before You Ink

By Leeanne Padowski

While tattoos are rapidly gaining in popularity, I would strongly encourage you not to get one. I work as a personnel manager at a large retail store. If you want to come to work for us and have a tattoo, you may be in for a surprise. Our company's policy states that anyone who works in customer service cannot have a visible tattoo. We are not alone in having policies like this, as many other corporations and the military have policies that restrict visible tattoos. A 2011 study by CareerBuilder shows that 31 percent of surveyed employers ranked having a visible tattoo as the top personal attribute that would stop them from promoting an employee.

Our employees with tattoos face two choices. Some wear long-sleeved turtleneck shirts to cover tattoos on their necks and arms. Others get their tattoos removed, a long process that could take many trips to a dermatologist and cost thousands of dollars. Tattoo removal is painful. It is often described as feeling like having hot oil poured on your skin.

Also, please consider the health risks of getting a tattoo. According to the Mayo Clinic, tattoos can lead to skin infections as well as allergic reactions that can occur even years after you have been tattooed. If the tattoo needle an artist uses is contaminated, you run the risk of getting dangerous blood-borne diseases like tetanus and hepatitis B and C. Tattoos can also cause keloids, raised bumpy areas on the skin caused by overgrown scar tissue.

Finally, please think before you ink! A recent study showed that two out of five people regret getting their tattoos. This includes Hollywood actor Johnny Depp who had the words "Winona Forever" tattooed on his arm in honor of his then girlfriend Winona Ryder. When they broke up, Depp was forced to erase part of his tattoo. It now reads, "Wino Forever."

Prompt

Mr. Johnson's article outlines the benefit of getting tattoos, while Ms. Padowski's article identifies drawbacks of tattoos.

In your response, analyze both positions presented in the articles to determine which one is best supported. Use relevant and specific evidence from the articles to support your response.

This task may require approximately 45 minutes to complete.

To read and respond to this prompt online, go to **writing4.newreaderspress.com**.

Planning Box

2: Minimum Wage

Let's Make the Minimum Wage a Living Wage

Ira Knight, speaking at a political rally, East Township, Maine, September 22, 2014

As a teenager, I worked at a local fast-food restaurant making minimum wage. It was a great job to learn customer service skills and build my work experience. According to the U.S. Bureau of Labor Statistics, more than 3.8 million employees currently work at minimum wage jobs. Some were like me, teenagers in their first job. Others were retired workers supplementing their Social Security income while still others were the working poor struggling to make ends meet. To help all these workers and improve our economy, the U.S. government should raise the minimum wage.

Increasing the minimum wage will help improve America's economy. A 2011 study from the Chicago Federal Reserve Bank showed that increasing the minimum wage leads to higher consumer spending, especially on car purchases. The study also showed that every dollar the minimum wage was increased resulted in $2,800 in new household spending over the next year. Another study reported that in the first six months of 2014, states that raised their minimum wage have seen more job growth than those states who kept their minimum wage the same. So instead of being a job killer as some claim, raising the minimum wage is actually a job creator.

Finally, raising the minimum wage would help America's working poor. A recent study from the University of Massachusetts Amherst found that increasing the minimum wage would lift 4.5 million Americans out of poverty. A 2014 study from the Center for American Progress stated that a minimum wage increase would remove 3.5 million people from the Supplemental Nutrition Assistance Program (formerly known as food stamps). This in turn benefits the U.S. government since fewer people receiving government assistance means savings for all taxpayers.

Keep the Minimum Wage Where It Is

Janice Steele, *Huntington Post,* October 17, 2014

It seems that every time there is an election coming up, politicians talk about raising the minimum wage. While this seems like it would help them, increasing the minimum wage hurts the very people it is supposed to help: workers. It is also bad for consumers, the economy, and small businesses.

Raising the minimum wage will prove to be a disaster for workers. Businesses only have a certain amount of money available to pay their workers. They will respond to a minimum wage hike by doing one of two things. They will either fire some of their workers, or they will give their employees less hours to work. In both cases, workers will earn less money at the higher wage than they would if the minimum wage stayed the same. A 2014 report from the Congressional Budget Office estimates that if the minimum wage were raised $1.75, more than 100,000 jobs would be lost nationwide. A $2.85 increase would cost half a million jobs!

Small businesses, the heart of America, will also be hurt. Most minimum wage workers are employed by small businesses with less than 500 people. The National Federation of Independent Business Research Foundation discovered that raising the minimum wage would see states lose an average of 47,000 jobs. More than two-thirds of these jobs would be lost at small businesses since such a large part of their earnings go toward worker pay.

Not only will workers and small businesses suffer, but a minimum wage hike will also be bad for consumers and the economy. Employers' cost of doing business rises as the minimum wage increases. To keep their profit margins, most businesses will pass these higher costs to consumers in the form of higher prices. As prices rise, consumers will buy less. This could lead to a recession causing even more unemployment for minimum wage workers.

Prompt

While Mr. Knight's speech outlines the benefits of raising the minimum wage, Ms. Steele's article disagrees about the effect it would have on workers and the economy.

In your response, analyze both the speech and the article to determine which position is best supported. Use relevant and specific evidence from both sources to support your response.

This task may require approximately 45 minutes to complete.

Planning Box

3: Violent Video Games

Violent Video Games Harm Our Kids

J. Ramirez, *Clinton Village News,* March 1, 2013

There is a direct link between violent video games and violent behavior in young people.

Sadly, the numerous reports of school shootings we hear so often are committed by young people who played countless hours of violent video games. Both shooters responsible for the 1999 Columbine High School massacre were devoted fans of Doom and Mortal Kombat, games that reward killing. The Sandy Hook shooter, Adam Lanza, loved the shooting game Call of Duty. James Holmes, the Aurora, Colorado, movie theater killer, also loved brutal video games. To prevent more killings, violent video games should be banned.

In addition to these examples, an even more direct link of video game to real-life violence occurred in 2006. Alabama teen Devin Moore was arrested by local police on suspicion of car theft. While in custody at the police station, he suddenly attacked an officer, stole his gun, and used it to kill two officers and a 911 dispatcher. He then stole a police car and made his getaway. Moore had no previous criminal record, so where did he learn this behavior? He spent over 10 hours per week playing Grand Theft Auto, a video game where players shoot police officers and steal cars.

Our armed forces definitely believe video games can be used to train people to kill. The U.S. military uses video games both to recruit future solders and to train new recruits for combat. Games like Virtual Battlespace 2 provide realistic environments that train soldiers how to kill. These games desensitize soldiers to violence in training making it easier for them to shoot to kill once in combat. Military trainers are quoted as saying that video games not only teach their soldiers what to think but how to think. So if our military thinks violent video games are powerful enough to teach young men and women how to think, we are truly kidding ourselves if we believe they are only fun entertainment.

Violent Video Games Are Harmless Fun

***Clinton Village News* editorial, March 9, 2013**

The article "Violent Video Games Harm Our Kids" tries to scare us into believing video games are destructive to young people. However, these video games do not cause violence in young people and therefore should not be banned.

There is no link between violent video games and teen violence. Between 1995 and 2008, there was an incredible decline in youth violence across America. The arrest rate for teens that committed violent crimes fell by half. During the same time period, video games exploded in popularity with sales today four times what they were in the mid-1990s. If those who say video games increase youth violence are right, we would see an increase in teen violence matching the higher violent video game sales. Instead we see just the opposite.

It seems that after every school shooting that occurs, the media are quick to blame violent video game play for the shooter's actions. In a 2004 study, the U.S. Secret Service found that only 1 in 8 school shooters had an interest in violent video games. Their interest in violent movies, books, and their own writings was much stronger than in video games. Harvard researchers found that for teens today, playing video games is a rite of passage, and only those young people who played more than 15 hours a week of violent video games showed aggressive behavior.

Let's give our kids credit for some intelligence. They understand the difference between fantasy and reality. They realize they cannot act in real life as they do when they play action-oriented shoot 'em up games. Instead of increasing violence, these games provide a safe outlet for kids to release their aggression and learn to control their emotions. In the past, alarmists thought radio, movies, and TV would increase youth violence. They did not, and violent video games do not either.

Prompt

The article by J. Ramirez links violent video games to youth violence, while the editorial outlines an opposing view.

In your response, analyze both positions to determine which one is best supported. Use relevant and specific evidence from the article and the editorial to support your response.

This task may require approximately 45 minutes to complete.

Planning Box

4: Drug Testing

Drug Testing Welfare Recipients Just Makes Sense

***Santa Fe County Gazette* editorial, January 6, 2015**

Each year, the U.S. government provides almost 1 trillion dollars in aid to low-income families in the form of welfare benefits. Programs like Temporary Assistance for Needy Families (TANF) and Supplemental Nutrition Assistance Program (SNAP) provide low-income recipients with cash assistance to pay for food, clothing, housing, and other needs. I strongly believe that anyone who receives welfare should be required to pass drug tests in order to receive their benefits. This will help make sure that welfare recipients do not use illegal drugs, welfare dollars go where they are supposed to, and welfare programs help save taxpayer dollars.

Random drug testing would help substance-abusing welfare recipients conquer their drug problems. It would identify those who need help and offer them treatment. Instead of paying them money that would be used to buy more drugs, substance abusers would not be given benefits until they stopped their illegal drug use. Being drug free would improve their chances of employment and better their lives.

Required drug testing ensures that welfare dollars will be used as intended, helping poor families get back on their feet. Illegal drug users must not be able to use taxpayer-provided government benefits to buy drugs. Instead, this money should be used to buy food and provide housing for their families. Creating a drug testing policy is really about protecting children. By ensuring that welfare money is used as it should, children will receive the food and care they need.

Drug testing will also save welfare programs money. A 2007 Robert Wood Johnson Foundation study showed that 20 percent of TANF recipients reported having used an illegal drug at least once in the past year and at least 5 percent admitted they had a substance abuse problem. As these drug users are caught by tests, they will be removed from welfare programs. Knowing there is a drug testing requirement will stop other drug users from applying for benefits in the first place, saving welfare programs even more money.

Say No to Drug Testing

***Santa Fe County Gazette* editorial, January 9, 2015**

There has been some recent debate about whether to require welfare recipients to undergo mandatory drug testing in order to receive benefits. I am against requiring welfare recipients to pass drug tests because it is unconstitutional, stereotypes welfare recipients, and does not save taxpayers' money.

A law requiring drug tests would be unconstitutional. The U.S. Constitution's Fourth Amendment protects Americans against unreasonable searches and seizures. In order to perform a legal search, there must be individualized suspicion of wrongdoing. An appeals court recently struck down a Florida law that required drug testing for welfare recipients. The court said that just because people apply for public assistance does not mean they lose their constitutional rights of protection from unreasonable searches.

A drug testing requirement also unfairly stereotypes welfare recipients. It assumes that if someone receives welfare they are more likely to use illegal drugs than the average American. Instead of looking at welfare recipients as people, it assumes all welfare recipients are lazy, illegal drug users trying to get government money to support their habits. In fact, a 2012 study by the Urban Institute shows that the majority of TANF recipients are children. So this stereotype of the typical welfare recipient is definitely untrue.

Mandatory drug testing programs for welfare recipients do not save money. A 2011 Florida drug testing law in effect for four months actually cost the state more. Florida spent more money on drug testing than it saved in the benefits denied to the only 2.6 percent of people who failed the tests. It also found that welfare caseloads did not decrease while the drug testing law was in effect.

Prompt

The editorials present opposing arguments on the issue of drug testing welfare recipients.

In your response, analyze both positions presented in the articles to determine which one is best supported. Use relevant and specific evidence from the articles to support your response.

This task may require approximately 45 minutes to complete.

Planning Box

5: Medical Marijuana

Medical Marijuana: The Cure Is Worse Than the Disease

By Jack Johansen, *Green Valley Weekly*

Those who support medical marijuana have put up a smoke screen of flimsy reasons to encourage its use. Marijuana is a dangerous drug that should not be used to treat patients' medical problems.

Since 1964, the U.S. Surgeon General has warned about the dangers of smoking. Yet the primary way marijuana is taken into the body is through smoking. It has been proven that smoking causes cancer and lung diseases. Compared with tobacco, marijuana smoke contains 50 to 70 percent more cancer-causing chemicals. To gain marijuana's benefits, users inhale it more deeply into their lungs and hold it much longer than tobacco smoke, which could lead to a greater increase in lung diseases like emphysema and chronic bronchitis. Would we have patients smoke opium to get morphine's benefits or ask people to eat willow bark to get the benefits of aspirin? Then why would we ask patients to smoke marijuana to receive its benefits? All these smoke-related dangers make medical marijuana more likely to cause disease than to treat it.

Beyond the dangers of smoking, medical marijuana has other risks as well. It is a toxic mix of over 400 chemicals, many of which have unknown side effects. It is a psychoactive drug that alters a user's brain functions. Depending on how it reacts with the brain, marijuana use increases anxiety, impairs thinking, and causes hallucinations. There is also the very real danger of users becoming addicted. Clearly, marijuana is a dangerous drug.

Recognizing marijuana's dangers, the U.S. government still classifies it as a Schedule I drug under the Controlled Substances Act. Schedule I drugs must meet three different criteria: high potential for abuse, no currently accepted medical use, and lack of safety for use even under medical supervision. Much more rigorous testing needs to be done on any supposed benefits before allowing marijuana for medical use.

Medical Marijuana Makes Sense

Letter to the Editor, *Green Valley Weekly*

Imagine you are a cancer patient and are undergoing chemotherapy treatments. While the lifesaving cancer drugs run through your body, they are also making you very sick. You experience pain, nausea, and vomiting and desperately want relief. Medical marijuana can provide that relief, and it should be used to help patients.

Medical marijuana has been shown in a number of studies to provide effective relief to the symptoms cancer patients experience during their treatments. Medical marijuana has also been shown to help AIDS patients in two ways: it improves their immune systems and keeps them from losing weight.

In his article, Johansen discusses how dangerous it is to smoke marijuana. While some patients do smoke medical marijuana, there are safer ways to take the drug. Some patients eat marijuana. Simple devices called vaporizers allow users to take in marijuana without smoking. Even for those patients who do smoke, short-term smoking has not been shown to be harmful. A chemotherapy patient who smokes marijuana for a few short months during treatments is in no medical danger.

Johansen also uses scare tactics to get his point across. Marijuana is a psychoactive drug but so are brain-altering substances like coffee, cigarettes, sleeping pills, and beer. According to CNN medical correspondent Dr. Sanjay Gupta, marijuana is not a dangerous drug; it was classified as Schedule I because of the lack of knowledge of its effects. He notes that studies about marijuana are biased, as more than 90 percent of studies focus on marijuana's potential harms while 6 percent study its positive effects. Dr. Gupta also mentions that fewer than 10 percent of marijuana users become addicted according to studies.

Prompt

The article and the letter to the editor present arguments for and against legalizing medical marijuana.

In your response, analyze both of the positions presented to determine which one is best supported. Use relevant and specific evidence to support your response.

This task may require approximately 45 minutes to complete.

Planning Box

6: Concealed Carry Laws

Let's Not Get Carried Away with Concealed Carry Laws

Leroy King, Horseshoe County Executive, speaking at a town hall meeting, November 12, 2014

Some states have concealed carry laws that allow people to carry guns not visible to others. These laws are a terrible idea for so many reasons.

Despite claims by supporters, concealed carry laws do not reduce or deter crime. A survey of convicted felons found they were more likely to use guns because their victims might be armed. A 1995 study of five major cities found that gun-related homicides increased by an average of 4.5 per 100,000 people in states that allowed concealed carry. Another study conducted over 33 years found that concealed carry states had increases in assaults, robberies, auto theft, and burglaries.

Instead of stopping crime, concealed weapons can take an ordinary disagreement and allow it to spiral completely out of control. Instead of a war of words or fists erupting over an argument, a gun battle can start. Take the famous case of Trayvon Martin in 2012. George Zimmerman, Trayvon's killer, had a concealed gun that he used to shoot the unarmed 17 year old after the two got into an argument. Or take the January 2014 shooting by a retired police officer with a concealed handgun who killed another man over an argument about texting in a movie theater. People carrying a concealed weapon are more likely to use it during arguments that otherwise would not end in bloodshed.

Concealed handgun owners are also a threat to public safety. While law enforcement officers receive extensive firearm training, concealed weapon owners may have little or none. Some states like Maryland require no training at all, while other states like Wisconsin require training, but do not specify what kind. In a shooting situation, do you really want to trust your life to a concealed handgun owner with no real firearms training?

Concealed Carry Laws Save Lives

Biyu Chong, speaking at a town hall meeting, November 12, 2014

Instead of more gun control, I strongly support concealed carry laws as they reduce crime, are our constitutional right, and prevent mass shootings.

It is clear that concealed carry laws reduce crime. A 2000 study of FBI crime data found states that allow concealed carry have lower murder, assault, and robbery rates. Think about concealed carry from a criminal's perspective. You probably would not want to risk your life trying to rob someone if you thought that person was carrying a gun. Detroit Police Chief James Craig agrees saying that concealed weapons are "a deterrent" and reduce crime.

Our right to carry concealed weapons goes all the way back to our country's beginning. The U.S. Constitution's Second Amendment guarantees citizens the right to bear (carry) arms. This right is so important that our founders put it second in the Bill of Rights after guaranteeing free speech. In two separate recent cases, the U.S. Court of Appeals said the Second Amendment "must be interpreted to include a right to have a concealed gun in public, to have it ready for use, and to have it for self-defense." Therefore, the Constitution allows for and protects the rights of responsible citizens to carry concealed firearms.

In addition to constitutional protection, citizens carrying concealed weapons are our best chance to stop gun violence. A recent *Wall Street Journal* article noted that it takes police officers an average of 11 minutes to respond to an emergency call. In Detroit, the average police response time is 58 minutes, which is enough time for a crazed gunman to kill many innocent people. A December 2007 shooting at a Colorado church was halted when Jeanne Assam, a volunteer church security guard with a concealed weapon, killed the gunman. Two people died in the shooting, but how many more would have been shot if Assam had not been carrying a weapon? In truth, the only way to stop a bad guy with a gun is a good guy with a gun.

Prompt

While Mr. King's speech outlines the reasons he is against concealed carry laws, Ms. Chong's rebuttal identifies the benefits of the laws.

In your response, analyze both positions presented in the speeches to determine which one is best supported. Use relevant and specific evidence from the articles to support your response.

This task may require approximately 45 minutes to complete.

Planning Box

7: Voter ID Laws

Point: Voter ID Stops Voting Fraud

By Angela Stampey

Dead people should not vote. Voter fraud exists in the United States, and our democracy is at stake when we cannot trust election results. To ensure fair voting, we need to require photo identification at the polls.

In recent years, we have seen cases of voter fraud that include individuals who used the names of dead people, impersonated others, and lived in the U.S. illegally. The U.S. Supreme Court has upheld the use of voter ID saying the risk of fraud is real and could affect close election results. In 2000, President George W. Bush won the election by only 537 votes. Every vote is important, and voter ID makes voting fair.

While some say that obtaining a government-issued photo ID is a hardship for many citizens, it is instead something necessary to have in modern life. Photo IDs are required to drive a car, get on a plane, buy alcohol, and gain access to government buildings. States that have passed voter ID laws also pay for people without photo IDs to have them made. In addition, several recent surveys have shown that less than 1 percent of the voting age public do not have photo IDs.

Finally, what about the claim that requiring voter IDs hurts minorities and the poor? Georgia passed a voter ID law before the 2008 election. A U.S. Census Bureau survey found that the number of African American voters actually increased after the new law began. In 2008, 65 percent of the African American voting age population voted, up from 54.4 percent in 2004. Our democracy works when people believe voting is fair, and voter IDs ensure this.

Counterpoint: Voter ID Laws Keep Real People from Voting

By Tavares White

I strongly disagree with Stampey's argument about voter ID. I am against requiring voter photo ID because it discriminates against minorities and the poor.

The lack of a valid photo ID presents a huge problem for many Americans. According to a 2006 survey conducted by the Brennan Center for Justice, up to 21 million American citizens do not have current government-issued photo IDs. This is especially an issue with elderly citizens over age 65, African American and Hispanic citizens, and those who earn incomes under $35,000 per year. Even for those with a photo ID, estimates are that about 4.5 million Americans' photo IDs do not reflect their current name or address. This especially affects young Americans in the 18-to-24-year-old age bracket who move frequently and are more likely to experience a name change.

Going beyond statistics, voter ID laws keep real deserving American citizens from voting. Consider the case of Pennsylvania's 93-year-old Viviette Applewhite, who is confined to a wheelchair, was a welder during World War II, and fought for voting rights during the civil rights movement with Dr. Martin Luther King Jr. She would be denied the right to vote under these new laws because she lacks the proper documentation to get a government-issued photo ID. Applewhite does not drive, had her Social Security card stolen from her purse, and lost her birth certificate many years ago. Is it fair to deny the right to vote to a deserving citizen who has been voting since 1960 merely because she lacks the proper ID?

The real truth is that state efforts to require photo IDs are not really about voter fraud but are led by Republican lawmakers who want to prevent minorities and the poor from voting. Since these groups are more likely to vote for Democratic candidates, stopping these citizens from voting helps Republican candidates win elections. Common sense and our history of living by the principle that "all men are created equal" tell us this is wrong and voter photo ID requirements should be dropped.

Prompt

The articles present opposing arguments on the issue of requiring photo voter ID.

In your response, analyze both positions presented in the articles to determine which one is best supported. Use relevant and specific evidence from the articles to support your response.

This task may require approximately 45 minutes to complete.

Planning Box

8: Fracking

Fracking: America's Energy Solution

Live at Five **transcript, Lucia Hernandez, February 20, 2014**

First, let me explain what fracking—or hydraulic fracturing—means. Fracking is a process that increases output from an oil or natural gas well. Fracking uses water pressure to break rock around a well. Oil and natural gas then pass through the openings in the rock and are pumped out of the well.

Fracking is vital to America's future. It improves our country's energy security. Today, the United States imports the majority of its oil from other countries around the world, such as unstable Venezuela and Iraq. Problems in these countries could disrupt our oil supply leading to higher energy prices. Increasing domestic energy production means that the United States does not have to rely on uncertain supplies from other countries and can count on its own production.

In addition, there are tremendous economic benefits to fracking. The oil and natural gas industries in the United States support over 9 million jobs across the country, equal to over 7 percent of the entire U.S. economy! The energy industry provides $86 million dollars a day in tax revenue to local, state, and federal government. By 2020, it is projected that the energy industry will add 1.3 million new jobs for America's workforce.

Speaking of economic benefits, how about fracking's effect on the manufacturing industry? Cheaper natural gas prices caused by fracking have sparked a manufacturing revolution in America. According to the U.S. Under Secretary for Economic Growth, Energy, and the Environment, "The increasing availability of U.S. energy at low prices has made many companies rethink their strategies of locating abroad, and others to return to this country." Because of lower energy costs, it is estimated that more than 1 million manufacturing jobs will be created by 2025.

While some people are concerned about the environmental impact of fracking, there has never been a recorded case of groundwater contamination from fracking. Engineers design cement and steel casings in each well to protect local groundwater supplies. About 99.5 percent of the materials used in fracking consist of water and sand and the rest are chemical lubricants. Companies carefully monitor these chemicals and either recycle them or dispose of them according to Clean Water Act regulations. FracFocus, a website set up by energy companies, details which chemicals are used in fracking and how local groundwater is protected.

Dangerous Fracking Practices Hurt the Environment

Letter to the Editor, *Salmon City Post,* February 22, 2014

Listening to Ms. Hernandez on *Live at Five* last night made me so angry! While supporters of fracking talk about the cheap energy it provides, they don't mention its real cost. Fracking is dangerous to the environment and should be stopped. It reduces our water supply while polluting our water and air.

Each fracking job requires anywhere from one to eight million gallons of water. With one-half million active wells in the United States, that's 72 trillion gallons of water used per year! This water has to come from somewhere. It likely comes from nearby wells, lakes, or municipal water systems, leaving local residents with smaller water supplies or potential water shortages.

Beyond water waste, fracking creates chemical pollution. Up to 40,000 gallons of chemicals are used in each fracking operation, containing a toxic bath of 600 chemicals like mercury and uranium. When the shale rocks surrounding wells are fractured, methane gas and toxic chemicals flow into nearby groundwater. Studies show that methane concentrations are 17 times higher in drinking water wells near fracturing sites. In addition, more than 1,000 documented cases of water contamination next to drilling sites has caused sensory, respiratory, and neurological damage to nearby residents.

There are other pollutants to consider besides chemical. Each fracked well requires 400 tanker trucks to carry water and other supplies to and from the site, creating air pollution. Fracking also produces waste fluid, which is left in open pits to evaporate. This releases volatile organic compounds into the air, which contaminate the air, soil, and water; make acid rain; and release ground-level ozone.

Fracking supporters like Ms. Hernandez need to get their facts straight. As I see it, no amount of cheap energy is worth risking our health.

Prompt

The transcript presents Ms. Hernandez's favorable view of fracking, and the letter to the editor presents an opposing, negative view of the process.

In your response, analyze both the transcript and the letter to determine which one is best supported. Use relevant and specific evidence from the articles to support your response.

This task may require approximately 45 minutes to complete.

Planning Box

9: Etextbooks

Memorandum

By Dr. Akua Adu, Sun City Superintendent of Schools

You may have heard on the news that our state legislature will be providing us with less money for textbook purchases. I propose that instead of using textbooks, our district use etextbooks, which are electronic textbooks the students view on a tablet computer. Etextbooks will save money, avoid the problems of paper textbooks, and help improve student learning.

Traditional paper textbooks are very expensive, have a short life span, and quickly become outdated. We spend almost $800,000 per year on textbooks. As state funding for education continues to decrease, we need to look for cost savings wherever we can. Average school textbooks only last about five years because of student wear and tear. In the time it takes to get books written, printed, and distributed to schools, their information also becomes outdated. That means many textbooks do not reflect current state teaching standards, and teachers must scramble to create lesson plans with current information. It is unfair to ask our already overworked teachers to spend their precious planning time doing extra work.

Compared to regular textbooks, etextbooks save money, are current, and aid student learning. According to a 2012 report from the Federal Communications Commission, etextbooks cost 50 to 60 percent less than regular textbooks. Textbooks can become easily outdated, and etextbooks can be instantly updated online, ensuring students get the most up- to-date information. Traditional textbooks only allow students to read them. Etextbooks allow for improved learning as students can easily highlight, edit, and add notes on the etextbooks, directly on the tablets. Students also have access to search tools and online dictionaries as well as the option to adjust tablet lighting to avoid eyestrain. A study by the U.S. Department of Education found that technology-assisted instruction can decrease the time it takes to learn new material by almost 50 percent. For all these reasons, the move to etextbooks will benefit our staff and students for years to come.

Sun City Schools Opening Session

Speech, by Keanu Williams

Dr. Adu and fellow teachers:

Call me old-fashioned, but we should keep paper textbooks in our schools.

When we count all the costs, etextbooks are more expensive. First, we'll need to invest thousands of dollars to ensure each student has a tablet computer. Then consider the expensive software costs and etextbook licensing fees. Let's not forget the needed upgrades to our district's Wi-Fi networks. How about the costs of training teachers to use these technologies and adding more computer technicians to repair and maintain the tablets? Tablets and ebook readers quickly become outdated, which means regular costly equipment upgrades, too.

I also foresee all kinds of problems with our students using etextbooks. I have never had a paper textbook crash, freeze, or get hacked. If a student drops a tablet, expensive repairs might be needed. Students seldom steal textbooks, but tablets are a very different story for a poor student interested in pocketing some extra cash. I found out the Algebra I textbook I currently use is not even available as an etextbook. Other teachers have told me they couldn't find their favorite textbooks online either.

We are all about helping our students, and etextbooks will not improve their learning. What about those students who do not have Internet access at home or those students who lack the computer skills for successful learning? In addition, tablets invite students to multitask, meaning they will pay more attention to apps, texting, and games than to schoolwork. A 2007 scholarly study analyzing students who read ebooks with hyperlinks showed how the links increased the brain's cognitive load. Ebooks made students more confused and they understood less of the material compared with traditional books. So to save money and for better learning, let's keep our paper textbooks!

Prompt

While the memorandum outlines the benefits of etextbooks, the speech presents an argument against them.

In your response, analyze the memorandum and the speech to determine which one is best supported. Use relevant and specific evidence to support your response.

This task may require approximately 45 minutes to complete.

Planning Box

10: Lottery Debate

State Governments Win the Jackpot with Lotteries

***Carolina Sun* editorial, May 8, 2014**

Lotteries are as American as apple pie. Historically, lotteries go back to Jamestown in 1612. Lotteries were often used in colonial times to finance building projects. The Continental Congress even held lotteries to help pay for the Revolutionary War. Today 44 states have lotteries. Lotteries are a great benefit for state governments as they raise much needed revenue, are a voluntary tax, and benefit education.

Since the Great Recession began in 2007, state governments have been scrambling to find money to pay their bills. State lotteries always provide a consistent and growing revenue stream. In North Carolina, lottery revenues increased by an average of 8.7 percent every year from 2007 to 2013 helping the state lower their income tax rate. Nationwide, lotteries fund about 3 percent of state budgets, a welcome income source in these tough economic times.

Instead of having to raise income or sales taxes to meet state budgets, lotteries are also helpful because they are a voluntary tax. This means that instead of being forced to pay taxes, people choose to play the lottery. Founding Father Thomas Jefferson is quoted as saying that lotteries are ideal money raisers exactly for that reason. People do not complain about paying money toward their state government when it is their choice.

Lotteries definitely help state governments to fund education. In Georgia, lottery money is used in three major education programs. Since the lottery began, more than $8 billion dollars has gone to the HOPE (Helping Outstanding Pupils Educationally) scholarship program. This program provides scholarships to high school students to attend Georgia colleges and universities. Lottery money also supports a pre-kindergarten program that helps at-risk students prepare for school success. Lottery funds also go to grants that help train public school teachers to use the latest technology in their classrooms. So while people play the lottery, Georgia students are the real winners!

States Lose with the Lottery

***Carolina Sun* editorial, May 16, 2014**

Instead of helping, lotteries are bad ideas for state governments. Just as most of the people who play the lottery lose, states lose too when we consider how expensive the lottery is to run, how it does not increase education funding, and how it hurts businesses.

While it seems that lotteries make huge amounts of money for states, they are very costly to run. Let's look at what happens to a typical dollar a state lottery receives. Only 25 cents of that dollar actually goes to state governments. Most of the rest is divided between paying out prizes to lottery winners (60 cents) and advertising plus administrative costs (9 cents). The remaining 6 cents is paid out to retailers (usually convenience stores) as a commission for selling tickets.

However, there is much more to the story. Cash strapped state governments do use lottery money for education, but the bottom line is that lotteries result in no increased education funding. If a state lottery brings in $450 million dollars, state governments take $450 million from their education budgets and use it to fund other areas. So while lotteries raise much needed income for states, schools statewide see no benefit from it.

The lottery also hurts businesses. People buy lottery tickets with money they could have used in other ways. Instead of spending money on lottery tickets, people could have gone out to dinner, to the movies, or shopping. So while the lottery takes in money, the restaurants, movie theaters, clothing stores, and other businesses see fewer sales. Victor Matheson, an economics professor at College of the Holy Cross, argues that lottery money spent instead with businesses would help create much more economic activity. Since Americans spent over $65 billion dollars playing the lottery in 2011, think about how much that potential lost income hurts businesses.

Prompt

The editorials present opposing arguments on the issue of state lotteries. The authors disagree about the lotteries' impact on raising money and helping education.

In your response, analyze both positions presented in the editorials to determine which one is best supported. Use relevant and specific evidence from both editorials to support your response.

This task may require approximately 45 minutes to complete.

Planning Box

11: Rent to Own

Rent to Own Makes Sense

A. J. Hoyt, Rent World Blog

You want that new HDTV and your smartphone needs an upgrade, but you don't have the cash to pay for it. You can charge it on a credit card, put it on layaway, or try to save the money. But credit cards charge huge interest rates, layaway means month after month of waiting, and who can save money when there are always more bills to pay? Rent to own solves all these problems and is the best way to get what you want now.

With rent to own, paying is easy. You are preapproved, so there is no waiting around for a credit check. Instead of having to come up with all the cash at once, you pay a little over time, usually under $25 a week. You control how you pay: weekly, semi-monthly, or monthly. There are flexible payment plans so you can change the amount you pay any time. You can also use an early purchase option and own your item now.

Rent to own means no waiting and no hassles. Just go down to your local store, pick out what you want and have it delivered at your convenience. That new HDTV can be in your living room as soon as tomorrow! Our trained staff will deliver your new furniture and even install your new HDTV exactly where you want it, when you want it. If something goes wrong, we will fix it or replace it for free, usually within 24 hours. Buying that same product in a regular store means picking it up yourself or paying a huge delivery charge. If the product breaks, then it's on you to fix it.

Finally, with rent to own you can change your mind. There are no long-term contracts. If things change and you need a new phone or a bigger TV, you can upgrade at any time. We realize that life happens. If you need to stop payments, just return the item and we will freeze your payments until you are ready to start again. With rent to own, you are never stuck with last year's model of anything!

Would You Pay 300 Percent Interest for a New TV?

Alyssa Myers, Consumer Watchdog reporter

Would you pay $2,900 for a $750 TV? How does being charged 300 percent interest on a new washer and dryer sound? These are the kind of deals you find at local rent-to-own stores. While rent to own sounds good, it is a terrible idea for most consumers.

Rent to own is the most expensive way to buy anything. A rent-to-own store recently advertised a laptop computer with easy payments of $19.99 per week. Buried in the ad's fine print, we find that it would take 65 weeks of payments to own the computer. The total cost would end up being almost $1,300 for a computer worth $585. This adds up to being charged 150 percent interest! Even making the same payments on a high interest 29.99 percent credit card would be $700 less expensive.

Rent-to-own store prices are much higher than other stores. Ads from rent-to-own stores claim a new smartphone has a retail value of $300, but we found it for sale at other stores and online for $125. A rent-to-own refrigerator the store says costs $1,000 we found selling for only $650. Even a rent-to-own store's "super spectacular sale" price results in consumers paying hundreds of dollars more.

Rent-to-own stores promise no hassles, but we found many problems with stores not explaining their contracts, encouraging consumers to rent more products than they need, and delivering damaged goods. Consumers who return products face hidden fees and stores use illegal collection practices like making harassing phone calls. The Better Business Bureau takes thousands of rent-to-own store complaints each year. Whatever you do, avoid rent to own!

Prompt

These two articles present opposing views of rent-to-own stores' payment practices, value, and ease of use.

Write a response that analyzes both positions to determine which one is best supported. Use relevant and specific evidence from the readings to support your response.

This task may require approximately 45 minutes to complete.

Planning Box

12: Studying With Music

Studying With Music Stops Learning

Dr. Phillip Ehrenberg, Psychology Professor, Our State University

As a member of the Faculty Senate, I am very concerned about our students and want them to receive the best education possible while here at Our State University. Listening to music while studying is a bad habit that interferes with students' ability to learn. To solve this problem, the Faculty Senate recommends that studying while listening to music should be banned in the University Library.

Walk with me through our library on a recent Monday night. There you will see hundreds of students supposedly studying. A closer look shows that students are far more engaged with the music flowing through their earbuds than with their books. They move their bodies in time to the music, caught up in a world far away from the thoughts of learning. The sound of music is everywhere. Students trying to hear their own music through all the noise crank up their volume, making it even louder. With all this music, the once quiet library has become a loud and distracting place!

Speaking of distraction, listening to music while studying contributes to the multitasking that is so harmful to students' learning. Students think they can listen to music, do homework, text, and use social media all at the same time. Research from Stanford University in 2009 and other studies since then all confirm people are terrible at multitasking. Since it is hard for the brain to determine what information is important and what is not, multitasking makes each activity take twice as long and causes 50 percent more mistakes.

Additionally, the music itself is a problem. University of Toronto psychologist Glenn Schellenberg found in a 2011 study that listening to fast and loud music interfered with reading comprehension. Ask most students about their favorite songs and most prefer the very kind of music that makes it hard to study. As reading is a major part of studying, listening to fast and loud music stops learning in its tracks.

Music Helps Me Learn

Shelly Nova, Junior, Our State University

The Faculty Senate at Our State University is considering a ban on students listening to music while studying in the library, claiming that studying while listening to music interferes with learning. Instead, listening to music while studying helps students learn and must be allowed to continue at the library.

Studying stresses me out. Thoughts race through my brain about all the work I have to do and about all the exams I have to take, making it impossible for me to focus. Music is the only thing that calms me down. Once I plug into my music, my stress melts, my emotions calm, and my brain gets ready for some serious learning.

Many students I know are easily distracted while studying or find that studying makes them fall asleep. For distracted students, music keeps them on task. They are less likely to look up and notice everyone who walks by their table. For some students, working a part-time job while juggling a full-time college schedule leaves them so tired that they fall asleep after a few minutes of studying. Music keeps them awake so they can focus and learn.

Finally, a ban on music in the library will not solve the problem the Faculty Senate is trying to fix. Students who need their music will just study in other areas. Instead of our quiet library, students will be forced to study in noisy dorm rooms or loud restaurants. The 2011 study Dr. Ehrenberg mentioned found that listening to music while studying was much better for learning than hearing loud background noise. For the sake of all the students across campus who need music to study, please do not ban music in our library!

Prompt

Professor Ehrenberg and student Shelly Nova have opposing views of students listening to music while studying.

In your response, analyze both positions to determine which one is best supported. Use relevant and specific evidence from the readings to support your response.

This task may require approximately 45 minutes to complete.

Planning Box

13: Vaccination

Vaccines: A Hidden Healthcare Harm

Mommy's Heart Blog

As a loving mom, I am very concerned about my kids' health. With all the recent publicity about vaccines, I must speak out. The truth is that vaccines are dangerous and parents should never vaccinate their kids.

First off, our children are given way too many vaccines. The vaccine schedule has increased significantly from 1983 to 2015. In 1983 the Centers for Disease Control (CDC) recommended only 10 vaccines between birth and 6 years old. In 2015, the CDC advocates 36 vaccines. Today, babies receive more vaccines in their first six months than their mothers did by age 18! The fact is these huge drug companies make lots of money on vaccines and have convinced the CDC to recommend more. Big drug companies are not at all interested in our kids' health but only in making a profit. Vaccines are now a $24 billion a year industry.

Vaccines contain substances that are very harmful to our children like aluminum, formaldehyde, and mercury. These toxic and poisonous substances have been linked to a number of diseases in our children including Sudden Infant Death Syndrome (SIDS), asthma, attention deficit/hyperactivity disorder (ADHD), and asthma. There is a well-documented link between vaccines and autism with more than 20 studies proving this connection. As the number of vaccines has increased, the discovery of autism in our children has increased right along with it.

Our kids are not developmentally ready for most vaccines. Babies receive their first vaccine for Hepatitis B when they are only 12 hours old! With the measles, mumps, rubella (MMR) vaccine, 1-year-old babies who weigh only about 20 pounds are given three live viruses at once. Young children's immune systems are not fully developed and receiving that many vaccinations at a time is dangerous to their health.

Much more rigorous testing needs to be done to convince me that vaccines are safe for my children. Until then, I urge every caring mom to just don't do it—stop vaccinating your kids!

Vaccines Save Lives

Blog Comment

Spreading half-truths about vaccines and children's health is seriously wrong, even on the Internet. The whole truth is that vaccines are one of the greatest advances in medical history. Vaccines are safe, effective, and all parents should have their children vaccinated.

Vaccines save lives. A 2014 study by the Centers for Disease Control (CDC) showed that vaccines saved more than 732,000 children's lives over a 20-year period. The study found that vaccination stopped the average child from getting four infectious diseases, preventing 322 million sicknesses across the US. This saved families an estimated 21 million hospital visits that would have cost more than $295 billion.

Vaccines do contain chemicals. However, they are present in very tiny amounts. Vaccines may contain trace amounts of mercury and aluminum but never enough to harm children. All vaccines are tested to make sure they are safe and effective before they ever are used.

Parents who believe that vaccines cause autism need to understand the difference between correlation and causation. More children drop ice cream cones on sidewalks in the summer but that does not mean summer causes kids to drop ice cream cones. Children naturally start showing signs of autism about the same time the measles, mumps, rubella vaccine (MMR) is given, but this does not mean the MMR vaccine causes autism. A large research study reported in the prestigious Journal of the American Medical Association in 2015 found absolutely no link between the MMR vaccine and autism in the patient records of over 95,000 children studied. In addition, health professionals have discredited the 1994 study that claimed a link between MMR and autism.

Let's stop the hysteria! The safest thing parents can do is to vaccinate their children. It will keep their children well and also keep kids around them from getting sick.

Prompt

These writers present arguments supporting and criticizing vaccinations. They disagree about vaccine safety and its effect on children.

In your response, analyze both positions to determine which is best supported. Use relevant and specific evidence from the readings to support your response.

This task may require approximately 45 minutes to complete.

Planning Box

14: Algebra Requirement

Algebra Equals Success

Shanae Stewart, Board Chair, Boswell County Board of Education

I speak tonight for all the children across our school district. We need to strive for the best possible education for everyone. To create a solid future, I strongly recommend that algebra be a high school graduation requirement for all our students.

Algebra is necessary for our kids to succeed in our rapidly changing world. Gone are the days when people could get good paying jobs that required little education. Our young people need to be ready to take jobs that have not yet been created tackling problems we do not even know about yet. The Georgetown University Center on Education and the Workforce predicts that 65 percent of job openings in the next 10 years will require education beyond high school. Algebra is the foundation for higher-level math. To get into and be successful in postsecondary education, our students must have strong math skills, which includes algebra.

I propose that our kids take algebra not because it is easy but because it is hard. Algebra trains the mind to think and to solve complex problems. Algebra is like weight lifting for the brain, making it stronger. Tackling algebra also builds character. When kids take on a difficult task and succeed despite the challenges it makes them mentally tougher and more ready to compete in our modern global economy.

To sum up, I recommend algebra for all our students because I want all our students to be successful. Telling some of our students that they do not need algebra denies them the tools they need to be successful. All our students need the excellent foundation algebra provides. Just as we all learned our letters so we could read, students must learn algebra to be ready for whatever the future holds for them.

I urge the school board members to join me in supporting a plan to make algebra required for all students in Boswell County.

Required Algebra: *X* Equals No

Priscilla Hanes, Boswell County Parent

I am no less concerned about our children's success than any member of our school board. I want all our children to succeed, but this is not the way. Algebra should not be a graduation requirement for all students.

All our students are individuals and unique in their own way. They each have different strengths, talents, and abilities. Making the same math requirement for everyone is taking a cookie cutter or assembly line approach to education. Our children are not cookies or toasters and their differences must be respected. Algebra is not necessary for all career pathways, so why should all students be required to take it?

Required algebra supporters point out that many jobs use algebra, but a 2012 study on workplace math found this was not the case. The vast majority of jobs only use up to sixth grade applied math (fractions, decimals, percents, and basic geometry). Very few jobs require algebra. Even most high-tech science, technology, engineering, and math (STEM) jobs do not require algebra. Most employers will train their new hires to do the specific math skills they will need such as machine tool math.

I strongly agree that our students need postsecondary education to succeed in the job market of today and the future. Yet requiring algebra leads to more high school and college dropouts. Some students fail algebra two, three, four, or five times. After that much failure, students get frustrated and give up. Failing algebra is the leading cause of high school dropouts and the primary reason that only about half of the students who start college earn a degree. Instead of postsecondary education leading to good jobs with wages that can sustain a family, students' college dreams die, and they are forced to settle for less.

I want all our children to be the best they can be, after all, they are the future. But requiring algebra for graduation is definitely not the answer.

Prompt

A supporter and a critic of a high school algebra requirement disagree about its benefits for students.

Write a response that analyzes both positions and determine which one is best supported. Use relevant and specific evidence from the readings to support your response.

This task may require approximately 45 minutes to complete.

Planning Box

15: Mandatory Recycling

Hope Valley Needs Mandatory Recycling

City Meeting Speech, by Sarah Lin, Mayor

The city of Hope Valley needs to be greener. By adopting mandatory recycling, we will conserve precious landfill space and save our city money.

Successful mandatory recycling programs stop huge amounts of waste from heading to landfills. The city of Seattle is an excellent example. Seattle's mandatory recycling program has been around since 2006, and statistics show it prevents 400,000 tons of waste from going into landfills each year. This is important because landfill disposal charges keep rising since the total number of landfills shrink each year as they reach capacity. No one wants to live near a landfill, so there is little new landfill construction.

Mandatory recycling also saves money. Estimates from Seattle show that city has saved $200 million in landfill dumping fees over the past 15 years since far less waste is thrown out. Cities also make money by selling recycled cardboard, paper, plastic, and metal. We estimate that Hope Valley can save $10 million in landfill fees while earning $5 million over the next five years selling its recyclables.

Finally, setting up and enforcing our mandatory recycling program will be simple to do. Only two things will go to the curb for pickup each week—a large blue recycling bin and a small garbage can. All types of recyclables will go in the bin—paper, plastic, glass, and metal. Enforcement is also easy. Recycling collectors will first warn violators by placing red tags on the bins of those who are not separating out recyclable items. After two warnings, households are fined $5 for each violation and multi-family and commercial properties are fined $50.

As citizens of Hope Valley and Americans, we should all be concerned about our city and the country where we live. Mandatory recycling is a simple way to keep our city beautiful and for us to live a sustainable lifestyle.

Hope Valley City Meeting

Open Mic Speaker Wilfred Grimly

This whole mandatory recycling idea is just plain crazy! That running-out-of-landfill-space argument is so overblown. Back in the 1990s, the Cato Institute did a study that found that a 15-square-mile landfill space could hold all the trash the U.S. would produce for the next 1,000 years. More recent studies show we actually have more landfill space per person than we did 30 years ago.

Mandatory recycling is costly. Cities that have mandatory recycling like San Francisco have seen their waste management costs go up. More expensive workers need to be hired to run the program. More specialized trucks need to be bought to collect the recyclables. More collection sites are needed and must be equipped with expensive technology. All this costs big money! Our taxes and fees are high enough now, so we certainly don't need more money coming out of our pockets to fund this.

Also, mandatory recycling is a complicated waste of time. I'm tired when I come home from work. The last thing I want to do is spend my precious time messing around in nasty garbage separating out glass, paper, and cans and putting them in all these different bins and cans. Who has time for this? I know I don't!

Most importantly, mandatory recycling is totally un-American. We are a nation founded on freedom, so we should never be forced to recycle. A government big enough to mandate recycling and fine us for violations is big enough to take over all our lives. What's next, mandatory teeth flossing enforced by the tooth fairy? The decision about whether to recycle should be our choice, and we should never be made to do it under threat of fines.

Let's take a stand, tell big government to back off, and not make recycling mandatory!

Prompt

A supporter and a critic give their opinions on mandatory recycling, landfill space, and the cost and benefits of recycling.

In your response, analyze both positions to determine which one is best supported. Use relevant and specific evidence from the readings to support your response.

This task may require approximately 45 minutes to complete.

Planning Box

SCIENCE SHORT ANSWERS

The GED® Science Test includes two short-answer items. You will be asked to read one or more passages and then write about them. On the science test, the passages will be arguments. For these questions, you will read a passage, graph, chart, or diagram. Then you will be asked a question about the material. Your response may be a few sentences or a couple of paragraphs.

To prepare for the test, keep track of how long it takes you to write your responses. The suggested time is 10 minutes for each short-answer item.

Science—10 minutes total

1. Read and analyze: 5 minutes

2. Plan and write: 5 minutes
3. Check and revise: When you're done, take a minute to read your response, check it, and correct it if you need to.

Each short-answer item will be scored individually based on the question and content. In the Answers and Exemplars that start on page 124, you will find notes about what a good response might include.

The GED test is given on the computer. To practice the Science short answers on the computer, go to **writing4.newreaderspress.com**. You can read and respond to a practice prompt that looks similar to the one on the GED test. A clock on the screen keeps track of your time. There is also a practice section where you can type your answers to the prompts in this book. When you finish typing an answer, send it to your teacher. Then your teacher can grade your answer.

1: Law of Conservation and Momentum

As part of a high school physics course, students tested the law of conservation of momentum. The teacher's plan was to have students work in seven groups that would use the same procedure and equipment, record the same measurements, and combine data. The lab room was small; only two groups could work on lab benches. There was room for two other groups to work on the floor. Three more groups worked in the gym, on a concrete pathway, and in the schoolyard.

Each lab group used the following materials:

- $ball_1$, steel, 25.4 mm (1 inch) in diameter, with a mass of 67 kg
- $ball_2$, steel, 19 mm (0.75 inch) in diameter, with a mass of 28 kg
- two photogates, lab devices that measure an object's speed

Each group followed the same procedure. First they set the two photogates in a line, 76 mm (3 inches) apart, and then set $ball_2$ between them. Then the group would roll $ball_1$ along that line, fast enough to move $ball_2$ but slowly enough that $ball_1$ would stop right after the collision. The first photogate would measure the velocity of $ball_1$ before the collision. The second photogate would measure the velocity of $ball_2$ after the collision.

The students collected data and calculated the difference between initial momentum (p_i) and final momentum (p_f). If they are equal, the momentum change shown in the table should be 0 or close to 0. The difference for trial 3 was 0.04, which is close to 0. The other results range from 0.15 up to 2.72.

Trial	Surface	Momentum change (*pi–pf*)
1	lab bench	0.60
2	linoleum	0.15
3	hardwood	0.04
4	concrete	0.82
5	schoolyard	2.72
6	lab bench	0.15
7	linoleum	0.26

Why did the different lab groups get different results? Describe how that could be prevented in the next group of pooled trials.

This task may require approximately 10 minutes to complete.

To read and respond to this prompt online, go to **writing4.newreaderspress.com**.

2: Fist-Bump Study

Fist bumping is a healthy way to greet others. Researchers in the United Kingdom compared it with both high-fiving and the more traditional handshake. They found that fist-to-fist contact spreads fewer bacteria. News of the study quickly spread.

The study was intended to help doctors and other medical professionals. They are exposed to germs from sick patients daily. It seemed like a good idea to study how germs may be passed on to other patients.

In the study, there was no actual skin-to-skin contact. The researchers had everyone wear plastic gloves. In each trial, one gloved hand was put into a container of bacteria. The glove was allowed to dry. Then the person with the germ-exposed glove greeted another person with a clean glove using a handshake, palm slap, or fist bump. The receiving glove was removed and placed in a liquid that collected the bacteria. Then the bacteria were counted.

The result? The fewest bacteria were transferred during the fist bump. More bacteria moved from glove to glove during the high five, since the palm is a larger area than the fist. As expected, handshakes resulted in the largest germ transfer. About twice as many bacteria changed hands in a handshake as in a high five. The researchers also reported that germ transmission was related to length and skin contact of the greetings. So it seems that longer periods of contact give germs more time to travel from hand to hand.

But is it really skin area and time that are important in germ transmission, or is something else involved? Fist bumps were the cleanest greeting. The other two greetings involved the palm. Do palms tend to carry more germs than fists do? Doctors' palms are a well-known source of germs that can spread what are known as "healthcare-associated infections." In fact, the Centers for Disease Control and Prevention (CDC) has estimated that 4 percent of hospitalized patients become victims of these infections. The *Journal of the American Medical Association* has even suggested banning handshakes in hospitals.

What was the hypothesis of the fist-bump study? Reword it to apply more generally to the spread of bacteria by contact.

This task may require approximately 10 minutes to complete.

3: EZ Slim Trial

A company claims to have a weight-loss product that really works and is amazingly easy to use. Just take three capsules a day, and watch the pounds melt off. You don't have to eat prepackaged meals, weigh your food, use a chart, or count carbs. You don't have to exercise. All you have to do is take one capsule with each sensible meal—breakfast, lunch, and dinner. The company published a graph showing the difference between a test group that used the product and a comparison group that did not.

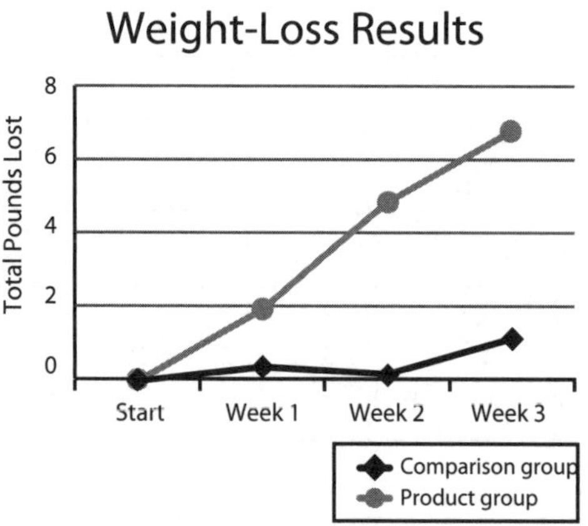

This sounds great, doesn't it? But are the company's claims believable? In advertising the truth is made as attractive as possible. But there are some questions a smart consumer should ask:

1. You don't have to eat prepackaged meals, but what *can* you eat?
2. You don't have to weigh your food, but how much food is a "sensible meal"?
3. Does it matter which foods you eat—as long as you eat a "sensible" amount?
4. Why don't you have to exercise?
5. What about snacks?
6. What exactly did the comparison group eat?

Other questions to ask are about the comparison group: What did they eat? How similar were they to the product group in age, gender distribution, and initial weight? Did they exercise? Most importantly, were they encouraged to eat sensibly, as the product group was?

What is one strength of this investigation, and what is its worst weakness?

This task may require approximately 10 minutes to complete.

4: Endocrine Disruptors

Endocrine disruptors are chemicals that may interfere with an organism's endocrine (or hormone) system and produce adverse effects. There are many possible endocrine disruptors in our environment, including BPA (found in plastics), dioxin (found in food products), PFCs (found in nonstick pans), and lead, arsenic, and atrazine. The weed killer atrazine has been used so much that it now shows up at unhealthy levels in surface water and drinking water.

Atrazine in pond water has been found to affect the larynx and reproductive system of male frogs. A group of researchers at the University of California, Berkeley, investigated atrazine's effects. They reasoned that atrazine might be causing the hormone testosterone to be converted to the hormone estrogen. This could be causing reproductive problems in male frogs.

A smaller larynx may have an indirect effect on frog reproduction. The male frog uses it to call females during the mating season. The populations of frogs and other amphibians have been shrinking for years. Could the decline be due to endocrine disruptors?

The researchers studied tadpoles in a laboratory. The tadpoles in the experiment were kept in aquariums, 30 to a tank. Room temperature, hours of light, and the amounts of water and food available were the same for all tadpoles. The only difference was that some tadpoles were raised in water without atrazine, while others were raised in water with atrazine.

The table shows the average measurements from all trials combined. The abbreviation *ppb* stands for "parts per billion." It means that *x* parts of atrazine were dissolved in a billion parts of water.

Concentration of Atrazine in Water (ppb)	Average Area of Larynx in Males (mm^2)	Average Area of Larynx in Females (mm^2)
0	0.086	0.060
0.1	0.101	0.078
1.0	0.088	0.077
1.0	0.074	0.052
25	0.078	0.060
200	0.088	0.064

The researchers determined that their hypothesis was supported by their data. The most significant results were found in males raised with more than 1.0 ppb atrazine in their water. In these males, the larynx was generally smaller than in the control males. Statistical analysis suggested a dose-response effect; that is, the size of the male frogs' larynx decreased as the concentration of atrazine increased.

Design a controlled scientific investigation of another suspected endocrine disruptor.

This task may require approximately 10 minutes to complete.

5: Fuel-Cell Cars

Like batteries, fuel cells generate electricity by transforming chemical energy into electrical energy. But unlike batteries, the chemical energy in fuel cells is stored in hydrogen gas. Energy is released when the hydrogen gas molecules are split into positive ions and electrons. The positive hydrogen ions bond to oxygen gathered from the air. The electrons are used for electric power. The only byproduct of this reaction is water. The only pollutant is some waste heat.

The hydrogen in a fuel cell can come from any number of sources. However, pure hydrogen does not exist naturally. It must be gathered from water or other substances, such as fossil fuels, which are rich in hydrocarbons. Energy must be used to separate the hydrogen from these substances. At the point of hydrogen production, pollution is emitted when fossil fuels are used.

Fuel cells are very clean at their point of use, no matter where the hydrogen originates. In cars using fuel cells, any pollution from the original source stays elsewhere, and the cars don't emit pollution as they are driven.

Powered by sun, wind, or another clean, renewable energy source, fuel-cell cars could be a real benefit to our future. But clean and renewable energy production is not at optimal standards. In reality, more than 80 percent of the energy used in the U.S. comes from fossil fuels. The car-loving American public is not likely to keep their fuel-cell vehicles in the garage while they wait for clean energy. If fuel-cell cars are developed, more hydrogen gas will be needed. But if more clean power is not developed, then hydrogen production will probably mean the continued use of fossil fuels. Nonrenewable energy will still be used, and air pollution will still be emitted. Development of fuel-cell cars may not be a good thing, when all things are considered.

What is the specific evidence in this text that fuel-cell cars are a good option for drivers who live in cities?

This task may require approximately 10 minutes to complete.

6: Hepatitis E

For medical researchers, one difficulty in sampling is determining the prevalence of a condition in a large population. The best way to do this may be random sampling. A number of factors affect the accuracy of a random sample, including the percentage of the total population you sample. Larger percentages result in more accurate results. But it's often not possible, or affordable, to use a large group.

One research group in England used their resources to estimate the prevalence of hepatitis E in the country's population. Instead of random sampling, they tested 225,000 blood donations given in southeast England over one year. This approach was relatively inexpensive and convenient. No additional resources were used to go into the community to obtain representative samples.

The investigators found that 79 of the blood donors had hepatitis E. They calculated the prevalence among the blood donors: 79 in 225,000 is equal to 1 in 2,848. They applied that information to the population of the country. The prevalence of 1 in 2,848 meant that perhaps 22,000 of the 63 million people in England carried the virus.

The researchers realized that the blood donors did not represent the entire English population. But they also knew that this type of sample—a convenience sample—was useful for exploratory studies. In the British medical journal the *Lancet*, medical researchers reported that hepatitis E seemed to be widespread in the English population. They also reported that the virus rarely made people very sick, but it was a danger to some patients with poor immune systems who received infected blood. As a result, the researchers suggested that all donated blood be screened for hepatitis E.

On the other side of the spectrum, the Centers for Disease Control and Prevention (CDC) shows what can be done when resources are not limited. Since 1957, they have been conducting the National Health Interview Survey. Every year, the CDC interviews thousands of households in a sample designed to represent the American public. The survey results are used to evaluate the health of the nation and to plan health programs. The survey results are shared with the public. Nongovernmental health and medical researchers sometimes use the survey results to conduct further studies.

What is sampling? How did it show that hepatitis E was widespread in the English population?

This task may require approximately 10 minutes to complete.

7: Narcolepsy

Researchers at Stanford University recently reported that narcolepsy, a dangerous sleep disorder, is an autoimmune condition. An autoimmune condition is one in which an organism is attacked by its own immune system. The Stanford researchers found that in narcolepsy, the immune system attacks and destroys the tissues that make the neurotransmitter orexin. Orexin helps people stay awake. A lack of orexin causes sleepiness in the daytime. It also increases the risk of falling asleep suddenly, sometimes putting people into dangerous situations.

The Stanford research showed that human T cells attack the brain neurons that make orexin. These T-cell attacks are stronger in people with narcolepsy than in people without it. Other research has found that T cells attack a particular protein fragment of the orexin molecule. That protein fragment is similar to one from a microbe that can make people sick. Narcolepsy sometimes develops after a bout of H1N1 influenza. It's the immune system's job to attack dangerous microbes. Any attack on the brain neurons is a mistake.

Stanford University is one of the highest-ranked science schools in the country. So the Stanford study got the attention of the scientific community. The researchers got just as much attention six months later when they retracted their study results. In the retraction, they reported that they had not been able to replicate one of their main findings. They did *not* find a stronger autoimmune response in T cells in people with narcolepsy compared to people without it.

Scientists are always looking for new, better information. And they must be willing to change their conclusions when they get new information. For example, peer-reviewed journals like *Science Translational Medicine* have other scientists review the research reports submitted for publication. These reviewers look for procedural errors and weak conclusions. It is also common for scientific results to be checked by other scientists after the reports have been published. Like the Stanford researchers, many scientists repeat their own experiments after reporting them. Retracting a study report isn't common, but it is part of the regular scientific process.

What data or evidence in the text supports the idea that narcolepsy is an autoimmune condition? What data or evidence in the text challenges that idea?

This task may require approximately 10 minutes to complete.

8: Projectile Motion

Projectile motion describes what happens to a cannonball after it's shot, an arrow after it's propelled from the bow, and a basketball on its way to the basket. The only force involved is gravity. This assumes there is no drag, or friction from air particles. Only the velocity of the projectile (cannonball, arrow, basketball) and the angle of projection have an effect.

Things that always happen:

- The projectile will quickly go up, then go up more slowly, stop going up, start descending slowly, and then speed up as it comes down.
- The projectile will take the same amount of time to go up as it will to come down.
- The path of the projectile, as seen from the side, will be an arch.
- The horizontal speed of the projectile will not change.

Things that change:

- If you change the projectile's angle, the horizontal flight distance will change.
- If you change the projectile's velocity, the horizontal flight distance will change.
- If you add drag to the projectile's motion, the horizontal flight distance will change.

Things that don't change:

- If the velocity and angle of two projectiles are the same, differences in mass won't affect their motion.
- Any projectile propelled horizontally won't go far.
- You can produce just as short a horizontal range by firing at a high angle as by firing horizontally (angle = 0).

Consider this example: A quarterback would like to throw a football farther. He tries throwing it at different angles, keeping the speed the same by using the same amount of force. A friend measures the distance of each throw. Another friend uses a protractor held at arm's length to measure angles. Their combined measurements produce the data to the right.

Angle (degrees)	Distance (m)
81	10.4
29	30.1
5	12.2
39	33.8
71	20.8
50	33.5
45	34.2
47	34.1
37	33.3
42	34.2

What trends do you see in the data? What angles produce the greatest distance?

This task may require approximately 10 minutes to complete.

9: Bicarbonate Reaction

Salad dressing is easy to make at home. You combine oil, vinegar, spices, and herbs. But you may find that your concoction is too acidic, which means that you used too much vinegar. A base can neutralize an acid. The most common base in the kitchen is baking soda. Vinegar and baking soda make a great volcano simulation, but not a good salad dressing. Another basic substance is antacid made with calcium carbonate.

What would happen if you added calcium carbonate to vinegar? Vinegar is acetic acid ($C_2H_4O_2$) in water (H_2O). Calcium carbonate is $CaCO_3$. When you combine them, you get calcium acetate (a salt), whose chemical formula is $Ca(CH_3COO)_2$, plus carbon dioxide bubbles (CO_2), and more water. Here is the equation for this reaction:

$$2C_2H_4O_2 + H_2O + CaCO_3 \rightarrow Ca(CH_3COO)_2 + CO_2 + 2H_2O$$

In any acid-base reaction, part of the acid molecule combines with part of the base molecule to make a salt, and the rest of the molecules combine to make water.

Note that there are two molecules of acetic acid: $2C_2H_4O_2$. If there were only one molecule of acetic acid, the vinegar-antacid reaction wouldn't happen. The reaction requires twice as much acetic acid as water or calcium carbonate in order to occur.

Chemical equations must be balanced. Notice that the number of atoms of each element on the left of the arrow is the same as the number of atoms of each element on the right. For example, the oxygen (O) atoms on the left add up to eight. There are also eight oxygen (O) atoms on the right.

A common remedy for an upset stomach is baking soda ($NaHCO_3$). When you mix it with a little water and drink it, the combination reacts with the stomach acid that's causing discomfort. Stomach acid is hydrochloric acid (HCl). The eventual products of this chemical reaction in the stomach are carbon dioxide, which causes burping, sodium chloride (table salt), and water. Antacids with calcium carbonate do essentially the same thing as baking soda.

Use standard chemical symbols to express the baking-soda reaction described in the text.

This task may require approximately 10 minutes to complete.

10: Kinetic Energy

The law of conservation of energy can be applied to a simple pulley to build a counterweight system. Masses A and B can be positioned so that they balance each other, and neither one moves. If neither is on a surface and mass B is larger than mass A, the pulley will look like the illustration below. Both masses will have some potential energy because of their height, and neither will have kinetic energy since neither is moving.

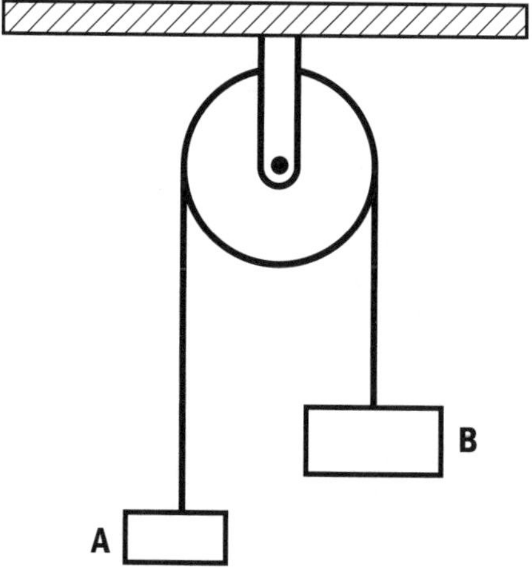

If kinetic energy is added to the system by a pull on mass B, it (mass B) will lose potential energy as it moves down. Mass A will move up, so it will gain potential energy. Another way to move mass B down is to cut the cable. Then all of its potential energy will be transformed to kinetic energy as it falls. (The same would happen if the cable for mass A were cut.)

You can also move mass B down by adding some kinetic energy to push mass A up. If you imagine yourself doing this, you'll see that it's easier to push mass A up on the pulley system than to lift it without the pulley. Without the pulley, you would be supplying all the kinetic energy to move mass A up. With the pulley system, you supply only *some* of the kinetic energy. Mass B's potential energy is transformed into kinetic energy to supply the rest.

In the early 1900s, a counterweight system was used in Seattle's electric cable railway. One route included a steep hill. When a streetcar reached the top or bottom of this hill, an attendant would connect it to a 16-ton weight on a cable that moved in the opposite direction of the streetcar. This helped the streetcar get up the hill. It also meant that less braking was needed when the streetcar headed down the hill.

Explain in words how a counterbalanced streetcar uses less kinetic energy going up a hill than a streetcar that is not counterbalanced. Use the concepts of conservation of energy and transformation of energy.

This task may require approximately 10 minutes to complete.

11: Toledo Drinking Water

In the summer of 2014, residents of Toledo, Ohio, were warned: Don't drink the water! Toxins known as microcystins had been found in the city's water supply. During the two-day ban, residents were told not to drink tap water, use it to brush teeth, or cook with it.

Microcystins are produced by cyanobacteria (blue-green algae). Algal blooms of cyanobacteria can occur when water is warm, sunlight is plentiful, and available nutrients are increased. The cyanobacteria multiply quickly and then die. Upon death, their single-celled bodies release microcystins. Toxic microcystins can cause liver damage by killing liver cells. In animals, microcystins cause diarrhea, vomiting, weakness, and death.

The nutrients that start the algal bloom come from a number of sources. Cyanobacteria use the same nutrients, especially nitrogen and phosphorus, that are used to treat agricultural crops. These nutrients are found in chemical fertilizers and cow manure.

Cow manure on farmland is usually considered an environmentally safer alternative to chemical fertilizer, because the nutrients in manure are released slowly. However, some farmers spread manure on fields early in the spring, before the snow has melted. The idea is that as the snow melts, the soil will get a mixture of water and nutrients that will increase the crop yield. But many of the nutrients run off the land into streams. When chemical fertilizers are used instead of manure, nutrient runoff occurs even without snow. Many streams join to form rivers that eventually flow into lakes, such as Lake Erie. In addition, the city of Toledo's treated sewage is released into Lake Erie. If sewage isn't treated effectively, some nutrients make their way into the lake from that source, too.

Toledo's water ban was blamed on an algal bloom in Lake Erie. But algal blooms have become more frequent in Lake Erie over the past several years. Microcystins have increasingly been found in water supplies around the world. The problem is widespread and serious enough that the World Health Organization has set a limit of 1.5 micrograms of microcystin per liter of water.

There may be many reasons for the increase in microcystins, but one is definitely the increase in phosphorus. Ultimately, two things cause the increase in phosphorus—the continuing growth in human population (around Lake Erie and in the rest of the world) and the never-ending attempts to raise more food per acre of land.

Assuming that things continue as described in this scenario, what can the citizens of Toledo expect to happen to their drinking water in the future?

This task may require approximately 10 minutes to complete.

12: Free-Body Diagrams

Free-body diagrams are used in physics and engineering to analyze the forces acting on one object at a time. Objects aren't found often in isolation in the real world, but this type of diagram is still useful. For example, if you wanted to determine whether the design of a bridge would work in real life, you could analyze each part individually.

When creating a free-body diagram, here are a number of rules to follow and symbols to use:

- An arrow represents a force. The head of the arrow points in the direction that the force is applied.
- A number and abbreviated unit at the end of an arrow show the magnitude of the force.
- An arrow and number combination is called a *vector*. A vector has both magnitude and direction.
- Two vectors can be used to represent force applied at an angle. One vector represents the amount of vertical force and the other represents the amount of horizontal force.
- The object under study can be represented by a square box.
- If a vector touches the middle of the box's side, assume that the force acts on the center of the object.
- The sum of the vectors indicates which way the object will move. If the sum is 0, the object will not move.

The box in the free-body diagram below represents a brick garden wall. The downward arrow represents the weight, in newtons, of a flowerpot on the wall. (Weight is a measure of the force of gravity.) The upward arrow represents the force that pushes up from any surface. It may seem odd, but the earth or a surface on it (like a brick wall) pushes back up only as much as a weight pushes down on it. They are equal and opposite forces.

To find the sum of the vectors, consider the upward force to be +80 N and the downward force to be -80 N. The sum of the forces is +80 N plus -80 N = 0. The wall isn't moving.

Which free-body diagram correctly shows an object moving only horizontally to the left? Explain why the other diagrams do not.

This task may require approximately 10 minutes to complete.

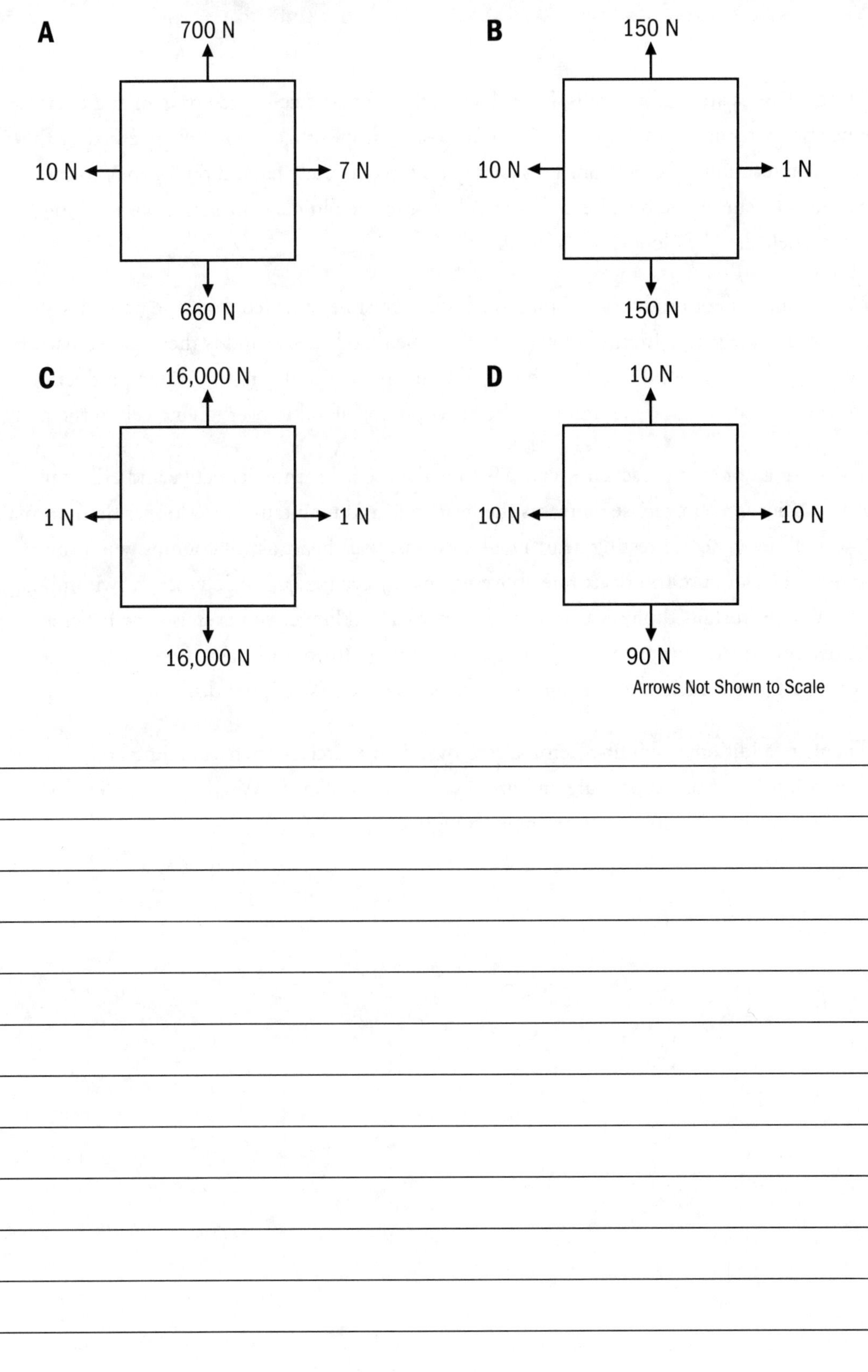

13: Exercise and Muscles

Muscle tissues are made of cells. Like all cells, these muscle cells need oxygen and energy. The energy comes in the form of ATP (adenosine triphosphate), which is released by the chemical reactions of digestion. This energy is stored as body fat and glycogen. Oxygen comes from the air we breathe and is absorbed into the blood at the surface of the lungs. It is then delivered by blood vessels to our cells.

Muscle movement produces carbon dioxide that must be removed from the body. The carbon dioxide passes from the muscle cells to the blood vessels and is then carried back to the lungs, where it is exhaled into the air. This energy use and carbon dioxide production are why we eat and breathe, and why the heart pumps blood to every living cell in the body.

The purpose of cardiovascular exercise is to make the heart more effective and efficient. Any cardiovascular exercise increases the heart rate and maintains it for longer than normal. "Normal" refers to the resting heart rate—how fast your heart usually pumps when you're at rest. You can raise you heart rate above normal by cycling, jogging, dancing, swimming, or any other sustained physical activity. The harder and longer you exercise, the faster and harder your heart pumps to deliver oxygen and energy to your muscles. Over time, your heart gets more efficient at the job. This decreases your risk of heart disease.

There are additional benefits. Aerobic cardiovascular exercises, such as cycling and swimming, lower blood pressure and improve cholesterol levels. Weight-bearing exercises, like jogging and dancing, improve bone strength.

Consider a specific cardiovascular exercise and a specific skeletal muscle, and explain how your heart's reaction during the exercise can make the muscle stronger.

This task may require approximately 10 minutes to complete.

14: Coral Reef Decline

Australia's Great Barrier Reef, which is more than 1,000 miles long, is composed of an uncountable number of small animals—coral polyps. An individual coral polyp is floppy and mostly transparent. Polyps take calcium and carbon dioxide from seawater and use them to build their very hard, and often sharp, partial exoskeletons.

Tropical corals live in shallow waters and have a symbiotic relationship with photosynthesizing organisms called *zooxanthellae*, a kind of microscopic algae. These contain pigments that provide the corals' colors. The polyps' exoskeletons are white limestone, but the pigments of the zooxanthellae living on them show through the clear bodies of the polyp colony. This does more than make the coral colorful. It also allows light to reach the zooxanthellae. Like plants, the zooxanthellae convert carbon dioxide (in the water) plus the water itself to sugars and oxygen in the presence of sunlight. The coral polyps feed on these sugars and give off wastes and carbon dioxide, which the zooxanthellae use to keep a feeding loop going.

These reefs are home to more than corals and their zooxanthellae. Many animals use the dissolved oxygen released during photosynthesis. The nutrients in the organisms and their wastes hold together a complex and large food web. Twenty-five percent of all sea life is thought to exist in and around shallow coral reefs.

Marine scientists are concerned about the threats that coral reefs face today, and they expect them to worsen:

- As the planet is warming, its ice is melting and sea levels are rising. The vertical growth of coral is not expected to keep up with the rising water. As a result, less sunlight will reach coral reefs, photosynthesis by zooxanthellae will decrease, and reef communities will suffer.
- Global warming includes ocean warming. Temperature-stressed corals tend to evict their zooxanthellae and become bleached. As time passes, more and more stressed polyps die, and the reef no longer supports its community of marine creatures.
- Global warming has been causing climate change, which includes storms of greater intensity than usual. Hurricanes have caused reef damage in recent years.
- Increased carbon dioxide in the atmosphere has resulted in ocean acidification—a lowering of the ocean's pH.

Name a human activity that can ultimately cause coral reef decline, explain why, and suggest a way to reverse the decline.

This task may require approximately 10 minutes to complete.

15: Air Quality Index

On a hot summer afternoon, it's not uncommon for the air quality in Los Angeles to be lower than in other parts of California. If you go to the EPA's AirNow website, you can find the day's air quality ratings for the city, state, and anywhere else in the country. The EPA's Air Quality Index (AQI) is based on a relative scale, with color coding from green (good) to maroon (hazardous). The EPA developed the AQI with the help of data from many experiments that tested health responses to different levels of air pollutants.

Rules exist to avoid putting people at risk in science investigations. To protect people, tests of hazardous substances may be done on lab animals. The lab animals may be harmed, too. For example, a lab rat may die when exposed to a certain concentration of ozone. Plus, that ozone concentration may have different effects on larger, different species, such as humans. So the information for the rat is extrapolated. That is, the information is considered along with everything else that is known, and then it is extended to estimate human responses to various ozone concentrations. The AQI is based on such extrapolation.

The AQI is just one of many limits determined by exposure-effect studies, also called dose-response studies. Others include OSHA's exposure limits to harmful substances in the workplace, as well as limits for harmful substances in everyday products that may be swallowed or absorbed though the skin. Dose-response studies are also used to do the opposite—that is, to find the dose of something that will get a good response.

For example, the exercise habits of more than 12,000 men were studied for 15 years. The data were compared and related to the subjects' risk of heart disease. This graph plots the relative risk (response) for men who played vigorous sports, according to the amount of energy they used exercising (dose). For most of this group, the risk of heart disease decreased as the amount of exercise increased. The most vigorous players didn't have the lowest risk, but it was still lower than that of the men who didn't exercise vigorously at all.

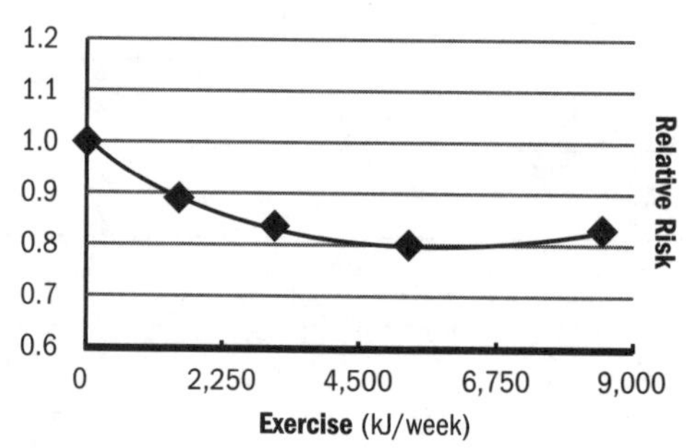

What is the dependent variable in this study, and what is its relationship to the independent variable?

This task may require approximately 10 minutes to complete.

16: The Fun Theory

Elmwood Health Department officials have been struggling with how to encourage people to exercise more. They know climbing stairs is good exercise, but they see far more people taking the escalator instead of the stairs when leaving Elmwood's downtown subway.

Elmwood officials heard about the Fun Theory. It claims making things fun gets more people to do them. They read about adding electronics to turn stairs into giant piano keys that play music when people step. Research showed this encouraged more people to take stairs, helping them exercise more.

There are two exits from Elmwood's main subway route, the East Exit and West Exit, and both have adjoining stairs and escalators.

Design an experiment to test the hypothesis that making the stairs fun to use will increase the number of people who will chose to take the stairs instead of the escalators. Include the following in your experimental design: experimental setup, procedure for data collection methods, and criteria for evaluating the hypothesis.

This task may require approximately 10 minutes to complete.

17: Single-Stream Recycling

Gianco Industries wants to encourage its employees to recycle more. The company has been using traditional multistream recycling in which each office has a regular trashcan and each hallway has a recycling bin with collection areas for paper, plastic and metal. It found that many employees throw recyclables in their office trashcans and do not use the hallway recycling bins.

Company leaders have read about single-stream recycling where traditional trashcans are removed from offices and are replaced by bins that accept all kinds of recyclables, including paper, plastic, and metal. These bins then have a small, attached bin for other waste. The company has eight offices, each with an equal number of employees, located around the country.

Design an experiment to test the hypothesis that using single-stream recycling will result in more pounds of recyclables than multistream recycling. Include the following in your experimental design: experimental setup, procedure for data collection methods, and criteria for evaluating the hypothesis.

This task may require approximately 10 minutes to complete.

18: Fracking and Health Problems

Hydraulic fracturing (fracking) is a method of taking oil and natural gas from wells deep inside the earth's surface. It involves horizontal drilling and then pumping a high-pressure water and chemical mixture into the ground to release natural gas and oil from rock formations and pump the liquids to the surface. Up to 40,000 gallons of chemicals are used in each fracking job to lubricate the wells and for other purposes.

Critics of fracking claim these chemicals seep into drinking water and cause health problems for local residents. Oil companies say wells are encased in concrete and that fracking takes place far below drinking water sources.

Residents living near Williston, North Dakota, claim they have suffered from a number of health problems (headaches, seizures, fatigue, and dizziness) since large-scale fracking began near their town in 2005. They believe it is because of an increase in toxic chemicals in the ground water due to fracking. The oil companies insist they follow Environmental Protection Agency (EPA) guidelines and that residents' health problems are not due to fracking.

Here are results from the EPA's ground water tests near Williston for toxic chemicals commonly used in fracking:

Ground Water Testing Results* near Williston, North Dakota

Chemical	1995	2000	2005	2010	2015
Vinylidine Chloride	.006	.008	.01	1.6	18.3
Sorbitol	10.2	11.0	14.3	25	91
Diammoniom Peroxidisulfate	1.1	1.0	1.0	1.1	1.0
Petroleum Distillates	2.2	2.1	2.0	1.8	1.9
Sodium Borate	4	5.6	16.7	218.3	9,413.7
Methanol	357	364	400	8,012	27,499
Propanetriol	8.1	6.3	7.9	12.5	56.7
Nitrilotriethanol	113	105	111	152	205

* All figures in this chart are in parts per million

Evaluate whether the data collected supports the view that there is an increase in toxic chemicals in Williston's water supply.

This task may require approximately 10 minutes to complete.

19: Climate Change

Scientists are concerned about climate change. One way they monitor our changing Earth is through global temperature data.

Two research teams are conducting a study using global temperature data from the Japan Meteorological Agency (JMA). The JMA monitors temperatures in 85 percent of the globe but has little data in the Arctic, Antarctic, Asia, and Africa. Some scientists believe the JMA's data collection techniques from 1891 to 1951 are inaccurate due to outdated collection techniques.

The research teams hypothesize that a rise in Earth's global temperatures above .5 degrees Celsius since 1880 is significantly above the long-term average and shows evidence of global warming.

Each team analyzed the JMA data and drew its own conclusion:

Brindom University

- They assume that temperatures in the 15 percent of the globe where the JMA does not have temperature data are similar to the areas where they have data.
- They believe that the data collected from 1891 to 1951 are accurate.
- They find that Earth's average temperature increased by .3 degrees Celsius and conclude that the Earth's warming trend is below its long-term average.

Phenell University

- They use statistical models to fill in the missing data in areas where the JMA does not have data. These models show the Arctic and Antarctic are warming twice as fast as the rest of the world.
- They corrected the data from 1891 to 1951 based on modern collection techniques.
- They find that Earth's average temperature increased by .8 degrees Celsius and conclude that Earth's warming trend is above its long-term average.

How could these two research teams using the same data come up with different conclusions?

This task may require approximately 10 minutes to complete.

20: La Niña and Severe Weather

Strong trade winds near the Equator create a weather pattern known as La Niña. La Niña cools the central and eastern Pacific Ocean, which affects tropical rainfall from Indonesia to the West Coast of South America. The changed rainfall patterns influence weather around the world. La Niña often causes flooding in Central and South America and an increased number of hurricanes to form in the Atlantic Ocean. In the United States, La Niña produces warmer than average winter weather in the Southern U.S. and wetter winters in the Midwest.

Meteorologists at the Severe Weather Center wonder what effects the higher winter temperatures and increased moisture will have on spring hail events and tornado outbreaks. After studying computer models, they make two predictions for 2015:

1. There will be more hail events and tornado outbreaks in the Southern United States than long-term averages suggest.
2. There will be fewer hail events and tornado outbreaks in the Midwestern United States than long-term averages suggest.

This table shows the long-term averages and observed conditions for three states in both regions:

	Long-Term Average of Hail Events and Tornado Outbreaks, March to May 1910 to 2014				Observed Hail Events and Tornado Outbreaks, March to May, 2015		
	March	April	May		March	April	May
Midwestern U.S.							
Texas	48	42	30		53	56	41
Oklahoma	25	43	55		23	40	59
Kansas	15	32	58		28	35	60
Midwest Total	**88**	**117**	**143**		**104**	**131**	**160**
Southern U.S.							
Alabama	19	37	55		26	45	61
Louisiana	10	19	36		14	22	47
Florida	24	42	63		39	56	78
Southern Total	**53**	**98**	**154**		**79**	**123**	**186**

Evaluate whether the data presented supports the meteorologist's two predictions about hail events and tornado outbreaks in the Southern and Midwest U.S.

This task may require approximately 10 minutes to complete.

RLA Extended-Response Scoring Rubric

Trait 1: Creation of Arguments and Use of Evidence	
2 points*	• generates text-based argument(s) and establishes a purpose that is connected to the prompt • cites relevant and specific evidence from source text(s) to support argument (may include few irrelevant pieces of evidence or unsupported claims) • analyzes the issue and/or evaluates the validity of the argumentation within the source texts (e.g., distinguishes between supported and unsupported claims, makes reasonable inferences about underlying premises or assumptions, identifies fallacious reasoning, evaluates the credibility of sources, etc.)
Trait 2: Development of Ideas and Organizational Structure	
2 points*	• contains ideas that are well developed and generally logical; most ideas are elaborated upon • contains a sensible progression of ideas with clear connections between details and main points • establishes an organizational structure that conveys the message and purpose of the response; applies transitional devices appropriately • establishes and maintains a formal style and appropriate tone that demonstrate awareness of the audience and purpose of the task • chooses specific words to express ideas clearly
Trait 3: Clarity and Command of Standard English Conventions	
2 points*	• demonstrates largely correct sentence structure and a general fluency that enhances clarity with specific regard to the following skills: 1. varied sentence structure within a paragraph or paragraphs 2. correct subordination, coordination, and parallelism 3. avoidance of wordiness and awkward sentence structures 4. usage of transitional words, conjunctive adverbs, and other words that support logic and clarity 5. avoidance of run-on sentences, fused sentences, or sentence fragments • demonstrates competent application of conventions with specific regard to the following skills: 1. frequently confused words and homonyms, including contractions 2. subject–verb agreement 3. pronoun usage, including pronoun–antecedent agreement, unclear pronoun references, and pronoun case 4. placement of modifiers and correct word order 5. capitalization (e.g., proper nouns, titles, and beginnings of sentences) 6. use of apostrophes with possessive nouns 7. use of punctuation (e.g., commas in a series or in appositives and other nonessential elements, end marks, and appropriate punctuation for clause separation) • may contain some errors in mechanics and conventions, but they do not interfere with comprehension; overall, standard usage is at a level appropriate for on-demand draft writing.

ANSWERS AND EXEMPLARS

Reasoning Through Language Arts
1: Tattoos, pages 6–9

EXEMPLAR RESPONSE	NOTES
In his article about tattoos, Ron Johnson discusses reasons why people should consider getting a tattoo. In her article, Leeanne Padowski argues that people should avoid tattoos. **Padowski's article is the better of the two <u>since Johnson is biased, and Padowski has better evidence to back her claims.</u>** Mr. Johnson is biased. In the first paragraph, he says, *"As a tattoo artist, I can tell you there are so many great reasons to get a tattoo!"* Since he makes his living by giving tattoos, he wants to see people get them. He is not concerned with giving people the most helpful information but instead wants people to come to his shop. His arguments are simply a sales pitch. Additionally, Padowski used better evidence to back her claims. The only evidence Johnson provides is a quote from a consulting firm CEO. The rest of the article is based around his personal opinion. He asks us to take his word on things like *"today's tattoo artists run safe and clean operations."* On the other hand, Padowski describes more solid evidence. She discusses a *recent study by CareerBuilder* about how employers would not promote a worker with a visible tattoo. Padowski also provides information from a *study done by the Mayo Clinic.* This study discusses the health risks of tattoos, a subject that Johnson almost completely ignores. Finally, it is clear that Padowski makes a better argument. Johnson is trying to sell people on getting a tattoo because he wants to make money. Padowski provides more and better evidence including two strong studies. Johnson asks us to believe his own word as a salesman without much support to back it up.	• The first paragraph introduces the topic. • The thesis (argument) is in bold. • The criteria for evaluating evidence are underlined. • Specific text evidence in support of claims is in italics. • Organization is shown through paragraph structure where first Johnson's evidence is discussed and then Padowksi's evidence is contrasted. • Transition words like *additionally*, *on the other hand*, and *finally* connect paragraphs together. • Awareness of audience is shown by writing in a formal style. • Purpose is shown in the concluding paragraph that summarizes the argument and reasoning.

ANSWERS AND EXEMPLARS

2: Minimum Wage, pages 10–13

LET'S MAKE THE MINIMUM WAGE A LIVING WAGE

Thesis: The U.S. government should raise the minimum wage.

Strengths	Weaknesses
Claim 1: Raising the minimum wage improves America's economy.	
• 2011 Chicago Federal Reserve study • 2014 Study on job growth	No source data on 2014 study
Claim 2: Raising the minimum wage helps America's working poor.	
• University of Massachusetts Amherst study • 2014 Center for American Progress study	
(This is the shorter of the two arguments and has only two claims versus three for the opposition.)	

KEEP THE MINIMUM WAGE WHERE IT IS

Thesis: Increasing the minimum wage hurts the very people it is supposed to help: workers.

Strengths	Weaknesses
Claim 1: Increasing the minimum wage will be a disaster for workers.	
2014 Congressional Budget Office report	
Claim 2: Increasing the minimum wage will hurt small businesses.	
NFIB Research Foundation study	
Claim 3: Increasing the minimum wage will hurt consumers and the economy.	
Logical argument on how the minimum wage increase could affect the economy	

ANSWERS AND EXEMPLARS

3: Violent Video Games, pages 14–17

VIOLENT VIDEO GAMES HARM OUR KIDS

Thesis: Violent video games should be banned.

Strengths	Weaknesses
Argument 1: There is a direct link between violent video games and violent behavior in young people.	
Examples of Columbine, Sandy Hook, and Aurora shooters	None of the three arguments have any scientific studies to support their claims
Argument 2: Direct example of Devin Moore shows link between playing a violent video game and real-life killing.	
Description of Grand Theft Auto game's influence on Devin Moore	
Argument 3: The military uses violent games to train soldiers.	
• Virtual Battlespace 2 is used to train soldiers • Military trainers quoted on how video games teach solders what and how to think	Quotes not included

VIOLENT VIDEO GAMES ARE HARMLESS FUN

Thesis: Violent video games do not cause youth violence and should not be banned.

Strengths	Weaknesses
Argument 1: There is no link between violent video games and teen violence.	
Decline in youth violence between 1995 and 2008 while video game sales increased	
Argument 2: School shooters had a bigger interest in violent movies, books, and their own writings than violent video games.	
2004 U.S. Secret Service study	
Argument 3: Our kids understand the difference between fantasy and reality.	
• Argument that video games help young people release aggression and learn to control emotions • Other new media did not lead to increase in youth violence	No sources given for the author's points

ANSWERS AND EXEMPLARS

4: Drug Testing, pages 18–21

DRUG TESTING WELFARE RECIPIENTS JUST MAKES SENSE

Thesis: Anyone who receives welfare should be required to pass drug tests to receive benefits.

Strengths	Weaknesses
Argument 1: Drug testing welfare recipients will help drug users conquer their drug problems.	
Logical argument on how drug users may get treatment, which would improve their ability to get jobs	
Argument 2: Drug testing welfare recipients will ensure welfare benefits are not misused.	
Logical argument on making sure welfare money goes where it should go	This is an appeal to emotions about helping children
Argument 3: Drug testing welfare recipients will help welfare programs save money.	
2007 Robert Wood Johnson Foundation study	

JUST SAY NO TO DRUG TESTING

Thesis: Just say no to drug testing welfare recipients.

Strengths	Weaknesses
Argument 1: Drug testing is unconstitutional.	
• Fourth Amendment argument that there must be suspicion for a search • Appeals court ruling	
Argument 2: Drug testing stereotypes welfare recipients.	
2012 Urban Institute study	
Argument 3: Drug testing does not save money.	
2011 Florida drug testing law	Law in effect for only four months

ANSWERS AND EXEMPLARS

5: Medical Marijuana, pages 22–25

MEDICAL MARIJUANA: THE CURE IS WORSE THAN THE DISEASE

Thesis: Medical marijuana should not be used to treat patient's medical problems.

Strengths	Weaknesses
Argument 1: Marijuana is usually taken in by smoking and smoking causes health problems.	
• 1964 Surgeon General warning • Marijuana smoke has more cancer-causing chemicals than tobacco • Users inhale marijuana smoke more deeply than tobacco • Logical argument about not asking patients to smoke opium or chew willow bark	• No source on marijuana smoke having more cancer-causing chemicals • No source on evidence that marijuana smoke is inhaled more deeply
Argument 2: Marijuana has other health risks.	
• Marijuana has over 400 chemicals, some toxic • Marijuana alters brain function	No sources cited on either claim
Argument 3: The U.S. government classifies marijuana as a Schedule I drug.	
U.S. government still classifies marijuana as a Schedule I drug under the Controlled Substances Act	

MEDICAL MARIJUANA MAKES SENSE

Thesis: Medical marijuana should be used to help patients.

Strengths	Weaknesses
Argument 1: Medical marijuana provides relief for patients.	
Studies that show it helps for cancer and AIDS patients	• No sources on the studies • Opening is an appeal to emotions
Argument 2: Marijuana does not have to be smoked.	
• Marijuana can be taken in by other ways than smoking • Letter counters argument that marijuana must be smoked • Short-term smoking is not harmful	
Argument 3: Calling marijuana psychoactive is a scare tactic.	
• Explains what "psychoactive" means • Provides counterargument to psychoactive drug fears • Evidence from Dr. Gupta • Provides counterargument about why marijuana is listed as a Schedule I drug	

ANSWERS AND EXEMPLARS

6: Concealed Carry Laws, pages 26–29

LET'S NOT GET CARRIED AWAY WITH CONCEALED CARRY LAWS

Thesis: Concealed carry laws are a terrible idea.

Strengths	Weaknesses
Argument 1: Concealed carry laws do not reduce or deter crime.	
• Convicted felon survey • 1995 study on gun homicides • 33-year study on concealed carry	• No date/source on convicted felon survey • 1995 study is outdated • No date or source on 33-year study
Argument 2: Concealed carry can allow disagreements to turn deadly.	
Two well-known examples of concealed carry leading to more violence	
Argument 3: Concealed carry laws are a threat to public safety.	
Examples from states show no or little training is required	

CONCEALED CARRY LAWS SAVE LIVES

Thesis: Evidence strongly supports concealed carry laws.

Strengths	Weaknesses
Argument 1: Concealed carry reduces crime.	
• 2000 FBI study • Logical argument about criminal's perspective • Detroit police chief quote	Credible source? Detroit has a bad crime rate and thc last paragraph notes their poor average response time
Argument 2: Concealed carry is a constitutional right.	
• Second Amendment right • Two U.S. appeals court rulings support concealed carry	
Argument 3: Concealed carry stops gun violence.	
• *Wall Street Journal* article • Jeanne Assam example at Colorado church shooting	

ANSWERS AND EXEMPLARS

7: Voter ID Laws, pages 30–33

VOTER ID STOPS VOTING FRAUD

Thesis: We should require voter photo ID in elections.

Strengths	Weaknesses
Argument 1: Voter fraud is a real problem.	
• Examples of voter fraud • Supreme Court has upheld use of voter ID • Example of a close election that fraud could have affected	No sources provided for voter fraud evidence
Argument 2: Photo IDs are necessary for modern life.	
• Examples of where photo IDs are needed • States provide photo IDs to voters that do not have them • Survey about few voters lack IDs	• Even if a free ID is made available, it could still be a hardship for a person to get it (travel, taking time off work) • No sources provided for survey evidence
Argument 3: Voter IDs do not hurt minority voting rates.	
Georgia evidence that voter turnout increased after voter ID law passed	Example from only one state

VOTER ID LAWS KEEP REAL PEOPLE FROM VOTING

Thesis: Voter photo ID discriminates against minorities and the poor.

Strengths	Weaknesses
Argument 1: Many Americans lack voter ID.	
2006 Brennan Center survey	
Argument 2: Voter ID laws keep real Americans from voting.	
Viviette Applewhite example	This is an appeal to emotions
Argument 3: Voter ID laws help Republicans keep Democrats from voting.	
Logical argument on why Republicans support these laws	No sources provided; sounds more like a personal opinion or playing politics

ANSWERS AND EXEMPLARS

8: Fracking, pages 34–37

FRACKING: AMERICA'S ENERGY SOLUTION

Thesis: Fracking is vital to America's future.

Strengths	Weaknesses
Argument 1: Fracking improves America's energy security.	
Logical argument on how increasing domestic supply means fewer oil imports from unstable countries	
Argument 2: There are tremendous economic benefits to fracking.	
Statistics on jobs, job increases, and tax revenue	No sources provided for statistics
Argument 3: Fracking creates manufacturing growth.	
• Quote from U.S. Under Secretary for Economic Growth, Energy, and the Environment • Estimate for manufacturing job increase	No sources provided for statistics on manufacturing job increases
Argument 4: Fracking does not cause groundwater contamination.	
• Counters argument that fracking contaminates groundwater • Counters argument about amount of chemicals used in fracking (99.5 percent water and sand) • Explains how companies protect the environment	No sources provided for how companies protect the environment; information sounds like it may have come directly from an oil company or other biased source

DANGEROUS FRACKING PRACTICES HURT THE ENVIRONMENT

Thesis: Fracking is dangerous to the environment and should be stopped.

Strengths	Weaknesses
Argument 1: Fracking reduces the water supply.	
Example of how much water is used	No sources provided for statistics
Argument 2: Fracking causes water pollution.	
• Examples show amount and type of chemicals used in fracking • Study about methane contamination	No information on the date or source of the study
Argument 3: Fracking causes air pollution.	
Examples of how fracking creates air pollution	No source provided on this information

ANSWERS AND EXEMPLARS

9: Etextbooks, pages 38–41

DR. AKUA ADU MEMORANDUM

Thesis: Our school district should adopt etextbooks.

Strengths	Weaknesses
Argument 1: Traditional textbooks are expensive, have a short life span, and quickly become outdated.	
Examples of three problems with traditional textbooks	
Argument 2: Etextbooks avoid the problems of paper textbooks and improve student learning.	
• 2012 FCC report • Examples of how etextbooks can be quickly updated • Examples of how etextbooks help students learn • Department of Education study on improved learning	No date provided for the Department of Education study

SPEECH AT SUN CITY SCHOOLS OPENING SESSION

Thesis: We should keep paper textbooks in our schools.

Strengths	Weaknesses
Argument 1: Etextbooks are more expensive than paper textbooks.	
Counters argument that etextbooks are being less expensive when all costs are considered	
Argument 2: Etextbooks have problems.	
• Examples of problems with etextbooks • Many textbooks not yet available in an electronic format	
Argument 3: Etextbooks do not improve student learning.	
• Examples of students with limited computer skills and no Internet access • Examples of how students will try to multitask • 2007 scholarly study • Counters argument that etextbooks improve student learning	No source information provided about the 2007 scholarly study

ANSWERS AND EXEMPLARS

10: Lottery Debate, pages 42–45

STATE GOVERNMENTS WIN THE JACKPOT WITH LOTTERIES

Thesis: Lotteries are a great benefit for state governments.

Strengths	Weaknesses
Argument 1: Lotteries provide needed funding for state governments.	
• North Carolina example of lottery funding • Nationwide example of lottery funding	No sources provided for either North Carolina or nationwide data
Argument 2: Lotteries are a voluntary tax.	
• Logical argument on how people prefer choice of playing the lottery over being forced to pay taxes • Thomas Jefferson supported the idea	Thomas Jefferson lived more than 200 years ago in a different time
Argument 3: Lotteries help fund education.	
Three Georgia lottery program examples	

STATES LOSE WITH THE LOTTERY

Thesis: Lotteries are bad ideas for state governments.

Strengths	Weaknesses
Argument 1: Lotteries are expensive to run.	
• Only 25 cents for each dollar raised goes to state governments • Counters argument that lotteries raise huge amounts for states	No sources provided for the data
Argument 2: Lotteries do not lead to education fund increases.	
• Gives example of how states treat lottery funds • Counters argument that lotteries add extra money to education budgets	No sources provided for the data
Argument 3: Lotteries hurt businesses.	
• Logical argument on how money spent on the lottery could go to businesses • Study from Holy Cross professor • Statistic on amount of money played in the lottery since 2011	No sources provided for the statistic

ANSWERS AND EXEMPLARS

11: Rent to Own, pages 46–49

RENT TO OWN MAKES SENSE

Thesis: Rent to own is the best way to get what you want now

Strengths	Weaknesses
Argument 1: Rent to own is better than credit cards, layaway, or saving .	
Outlines why rent to own is better than credit cards, layaway, or saving	This is written by a blogger working for a rent-to-own store so the writer is biased in favor of rent to own.
Argument 2: Paying is easy with rent to own.	
Highlights easy preapproval and payment options	• Does not explain what pre-approved means • Does not tell how long payments last or what the interest rate would be
Argument 3: There is no waiting or hassles with rent to own.	
• Highlights that one can get the item they want now • Makes easy delivery/ replacement sound good by comparing it to buying at other stores	
Argument 4: You can change your mind with rent to own.	
Shows how easy it is to change the terms of the rent-to-own agreement	Does not mention what fees or interest may be charged to change the agreement

WOULD YOU PAY 300 PERCENT INTEREST FOR A NEW TV?

Thesis: Rent to own is a terrible idea for most consumers

Strengths	Weaknesses
Argument 1: Rent to own is the most expensive way to buy anything.	
• Gives a specific example from a rent-to-own ad • Counters argument that rent to own is better than using credit cards	
Argument 2: Rent-to-own store prices are higher than other stores.	
Uses specific ads to show rent-to-own stores have higher prices than other stores	Does not specifically mention where the cheaper prices were found
Argument 3: There are many problems with rent-to-own stores.	
• Gives specific examples of problems found with rent-to-own stores • Mentions that the Better Business Bureau (BBB) takes thousands of complaints	Just said the BBB takes complaints, does not mention if the complaints were justified

ANSWERS AND EXEMPLARS

12: Studying With Music, pages 50–53

STUDYING WITH MUSIC STOPS LEARNING

Thesis: Listening to music while studying is a bad habit that interferes with students' ability to learn.

Strengths	Weaknesses
Argument 1: The library is noisy because of students playing music.	
Personal observation based on a visit to the library and hearing all the noise	A one night observation does not mean the library is always like this
Argument 2: Listening to music is part of multitasking that hurts students' learning.	
Recent study from an unbiased university about multitasking's bad effects	
Argument 3: Fast and loud music interferes with learning.	
Recent study from an unbiased university about fast and loud music	

MUSIC HELPS ME LEARN

Thesis: Listening to music while studying helps students learn and must be allowed to continue at the library.

Strengths	Weaknesses
Argument 1: Music calms me so I can study.	
Personal example showing how music calms her down	Is only using herself as an example, other students may not feel that way
Argument 2: Music keeps students on task and awake.	
Provides specific examples of how music keeps certain students focused and awake	The author only knows a small number of students and cannot speak for all students
Argument 3: Banning music in the library will not solve the problem.	
Describes a recent study from an unbiased university that shows listening to music is better than loud background noise	Guesses what students may do (study in loud areas), does not prove what they will do

ANSWERS AND EXEMPLARS

13: Vaccinations, pages 54–57

VACCINES: A HIDDEN HEALTHCARE HARM

Thesis: Parents should never vaccinate their kids.

Strengths	Weaknesses
Argument 1: Children are given too many vaccines.	
Information from the CDC showing the increase in the shot schedule	• No sources for claims about drug companies influencing the CDC • No sources for information about drug company profits
Argument 2: Vaccines contain harmful substances.	
• Claims a link between vaccines and harmful childhood diseases • Mentions 20 studies showing a link between vaccines and autism	• No sources provided for the link between vaccine chemicals and diseases • No sources provided for the 20 studies that show an autism connection
Argument 3: Kids are not developmentally ready for vaccines.	
Provides a logical argument about kids not being developmentally ready for vaccines	No sources provided for this claim

VACCINES SAVE LIVES

Thesis: All parents should have their children vaccinated.

Strengths	Weaknesses
Argument 1: Vaccines save lives and prevent illness.	
A recent study from an unbiased government agency showing vaccine's positive effects	
Argument 2: Vaccines contain small doses of chemicals but are safe.	
Counters argument about chemicals in vaccines being unsafe	Admits there are potentially dangerous chemicals in vaccines
Argument 3: The correlation between MMR and autism does not mean the vaccine causes autism.	
• Uses logic to show that just because two things are related does not mean that one causes the other to happen • 2015 study from the American Medical Association, recent study from a reliable source • Discredits the 1994 study on vaccines and autism	No source information about how the 1994 autism study was discredited

ANSWERS AND EXEMPLARS

14: Algebra Requirement, pages 58–61

ALGEBRA EQUALS SUCCESS

Thesis: Algebra should be a graduation requirement for all students.

Strengths	Weaknesses
Argument 1: Algebra is necessary for kids to succeed in a changing world.	
• Claim about the changing work force • Georgetown University data on the importance of education for future job openings • Claim that algebra is needed for higher level and postsecondary math	• No source data for the information on the changing workforce • No source data for the information about higher level math and postsecondary education
Argument 2: Since algebra is hard it helps students learn to think and builds character.	
Claim that taking algebra helps students learn to think and builds their character	No source information for this claim
Argument 3: Algebra helps all kids be successful.	
Logical claim that algebra gives students the tools to be successful	No source information for this claim

X EQUALS NO

Thesis: Algebra should not be a graduation requirement for all students.

Strengths	Weaknesses
Argument 1: We should not treat all students the same way.	
• Makes logical claim that all students are unique so they should not all be treated the same • Claim that all career pathways do not require algebra	No source information for the career pathways claim
Argument 2: Most jobs do not need algebra.	
Recent study on workplace math	No source information for the 2012 study on workplace math
Argument 3: Requiring algebra causes students to drop out of high school and college.	
Makes logical claim that algebra causes students to drop out of high school and college	No source information for claim about high school and college dropouts

ANSWERS AND EXEMPLARS

15: Mandatory Recycling, pages 62–65

EXEMPLAR RESPONSE	NOTES
In her speech, Mayor Lin argues that the city of Hope Valley should adopt mandatory recycling because it saves landfill space, saves money, and is easy to do. Mr. Grimly, however, says that mandatory recycling is a bad idea because it is an expensive waste of time and un-American. **Mayor Lin's speech is the better of the two arguments because <u>she uses logical arguments based on statistics and a model from a successful recycling program</u>.** Mr. Grimly just seems to be making an emotional rant. Mayor Lin carefully builds her argument through logic supported by statistics. She uses the model of Seattle's successful mandatory recycling program. She *cites statistics from Seattle showing how much less landfill waste there will be* using mandatory recycling. The mayor also *shows estimates of how much money Hope Valley can save and earn through recycling*. She also describes *how easy the program would be to operate and enforce*. Hearing the mayor's clear and simple plan that she supports with facts and statistics gives me confidence that the mandatory recycling plan will be best for Hope Valley. Instead of a strong argument backed by fact, Mr. Grimly's speech is only based on his opinions. He points to *increased costs with San Francisco's recycling program* but never tells where he received his source information. Mr. Grimly does *mention a study from the Cato Institute* but since it was *from the 1990s* that information could be 25 years out of date. He mentions *more recent studies* but again gives no information about his sources. Without any proof he is really just asking us to take his word for it. Additionally, much of Mr. Grimly's speech seems to be a rant. He uses emotional phrases like "*just plain crazy*" instead of building an argument. Mr. Grimly thinks that *mandatory recycling is only the first step in a complete government takeover of people's freedom*. He believes *mandatory recycling will eventually result in the government requiring people to floss their teeth with the tooth fairy enforcing the law*. This is a huge claim, which Mr. Grimly cannot back up with any logical evidence. Finally, it is clear that Mayor Lin's argument is far better than Mr. Grimly's. She builds logical arguments using facts and statistics. Mr. Grimly just uses emotions and his own opinion. If I lived in Hope Valley and heard these two speeches, I would definitely side with Ms. Lin and support mandatory recycling because of her stronger speech.	• The first paragraph introduces the argument • The thesis (argument) is in bold • The criteria for evaluating evidence are underlined • Specific evidence from the text is in italics • Organization is shown through body paragraphs where first Mayor Lin's argument is discussed and then Mr. Grimly's argument • Transition words like *instead*, *additionally*, and *finally* connect paragraphs together • Evidence from the passages are paraphrased (put in the writer's own words) • The essay has five paragraphs and 405 words • Awareness of audience and purpose is shown by a conclusion which summarizes the argument

ANSWERS AND EXEMPLARS

Science

1: Law of Conservation and Momentum, pages 68–69

Sample response: The data table shows that the largest loss of momentum occurred in the schoolyard trial. The next largest loss was in the trial on concrete. So the smoothness (lack of friction) of the surface seems important. Next time, all the trials should use the same type of surface. Maybe they could use a surface like an air hockey table, where there is little friction. It could also help to use equipment that would give $ball_1$ a reliable velocity. This would ensure that it stops immediately and transfers all its momentum to $ball_2$. It would also control the ball's direction, so all of its momentum would be transferred along a straight line.

2: Fist-Bump Study, pages 70–71

Sample response: The original hypothesis: Handshakes transfer more bacteria than do high fives or fist bumps. A more general hypothesis would be that more bacteria are transferred with longer person-to-person contact, or more bacteria are transferred with more surface area contact.

3: EZ Slim Trial, pages 72–73

Sample response: A strength was that the investigators used a control group for comparison (product vs. no product). The greatest weakness was that there were not actually two conditions but at least three: (1) use the product and eat sensibly, (2) don't use the product but eat sensibly, and (3) don't use the product and eat as you like. If the third condition, rather than the second, applied to the comparison group, then there was at least one confounding variable (i.e., a condition that should have been the same for both groups, but wasn't).

4: Endocrine Disruptors, pages 74–75

Sample response: The design will likely be modeled on the atrazine investigation and focus on one of the possible endocrine disruptors mentioned. Designs should include the following: a testable hypothesis with a defined independent variable (one changed by the researcher, e.g., BPA or no BPA) and a dependent variable (the results, e.g., larynx area); information on methods and materials (e.g., 30 tadpoles to an aquarium); information on controlled variables (conditions kept the same in all the groups, e.g., temperature, light); and a blank data table for recording observations.

5: Fuel-Cell Cars, pages 76–77

Sample response: Fuel-cell cars emit no pollution as they're driven. The only byproduct of the fuel-cell reaction is water. This could be a real benefit in many cities where there is already too much air pollution.

6: Hepatitis E, pages 78–79

Sample response: Sampling is the selection of a representative part (the sample) of a larger group (e.g., a population) with the goal of learning something that can be applied to the larger group. The sampling technique used in the English study was convenience sampling, not random. Though not as accurate as random sampling, convenience sampling allowed the investigators to estimate the general prevalence of the virus.

7: Narcolepsy, pages 80–81

Sample response: Support: The text says the Stanford researchers found that the immune system's T cells attack and destroy the brain neurons that make orexin, and that these attacks are stronger in people with narcolepsy than in people without it. Also, other research has found that T cells attack a particular protein fragment that is similar to a protein fragment from a microbe that can make the body sick. Challenge: The test says the Stanford researchers ran the experiment again but did not find a stronger autoimmune response in T cells in people with narcolepsy than in people without it.

8: Projectile Motion, pages 82–83

Sample response: The distance is small when the angle is either very small or very large. Angles between about 40 and 50 degrees produce the greatest distance.

9: Bicarbonate Reaction, pages 84–85

$NaHCO_3 + H_2O + HCl \rightarrow NaCl + 2H_2O + CO_2$

or

$NaHCO_3 + HCl \rightarrow NaCl + H_2O + CO_2$

10: Kinetic Energy, pages 86–87

Sample response: The counterbalance is a mass attached to a cable that goes over a pulley and is attached to the streetcar. The mass is at the top of the hill when the streetcar is at the bottom. The mass has potential energy due to its position. As the streetcar moves up, the mass moves down because of gravity. As it moves down, the mass loses potential energy and gains kinetic energy, because energy is conserved. Kinetic energy in the pulley system also pulls the streetcar up the hill. A certain amount of work must be done to get the streetcar up the hill. Some of that work is done by the kinetic energy of the cable system, so less electrical energy is needed.

11: Toledo Drinking Water, pages 88–89

Sample response: Toledo's population will probably increase, so there will be even more nutrients going into Lake Erie. The result will likely be that toxic water alerts will be more frequent.

12: Free-Body Diagrams, pages 90–91

Sample response: Option B shows the object moving only horizontally to the left. Option A shows an object moving both left and up. Option C shows an object that is not moving, because all forces sum to 0. Option D shows an object moving straight down because the sum of the horizontal forces is 0 but the sum of the vertical forces is -80 N.

13: Exercise and Muscles, pages 92–93

Sample response: Running stairs at the stadium for 20 minutes a day will increase my heart rate for at least 20 minutes. This will pump more than normal amounts of oxygen and energy to my calf muscles, which will allow them to work harder. It will also remove larger amounts of carbon dioxide from the muscles, allowing them to work longer. Muscle becomes stronger with use, so the cardiovascular exercise will strengthen my calf muscles.

14: Coral Reef Decline, pages 94–95

Sample response: Power generation has resulted in more carbon dioxide pollution, resulting in fast sea-level and temperature changes as well as storms of greater intensity and ocean acidification. We could reverse the coral decline by generating power in cleaner ways, such as with solar and wind energy.

15: Air Quality Index, pages 96–97

Sample response: The dependent variable is the relative risk of heart disease. The dependent variable *depends* on the independent variable. Here the risk depends on the energy expended in vigorous exercise. (The trend is that the risk decreases as expended energy increases, for most of the energy values.)

16: The Fun Theory, pages 98–99

Experimental setup: The hypothesis is that making the stairs fun to use by turning them into piano keys will increase the number of people taking the stairs instead of the escalator. Turn either the East Exit or West Exit stairs into giant piano keys as the experimental group, and leave the other exit unchanged as the control group.

Procedure for data collection: Have researchers at both exits count the total number of people who take the stairs and the number of people who take the escalator over a two-week period.

Criteria for hypothesis evaluation: Compare the total number of people taking the stairs to the number who choose the escalator at the East and West exits. If more people take the stairs at the exit with the piano key stairway, the hypothesis that making the stairs fun to use is correct.

17: Single-Stream Recycling, pages 100–101

Experimental setup: The hypothesis is that single-stream recycling results in more total pounds of recycling than multistream recycling. Since all the company's locations have an equal number of employees, choose two of the offices at random to conduct an experiment. One office will be the control group and will continue with multistream recycling. Another office will be the experimental group and have their office trashcans removed and replaced by the single-stream recycling bin.

Procedure for data collection: Have both the control and experimental office collect and weigh the total amount of recycled paper, plastic, and metal for one month.

Criteria for hypothesis evaluation: Compare the total amounts of recyclables from the single-stream and multi-stream recycling to see which system results in a greater amount of recycling. If there were more total pounds of recycling from single-stream recycling, the hypothesis is correct.

18: Fracking and Health Problems, pages 108–109

Of the eight chemicals shown in the table, six show large increases in the period from 2005 to 2015:

Vinylidine Chloride	Methanol
Sorbitol	Propanetriol
Sodium Borate	Nitrilotriethanol

This supports the view that there are higher levels of toxic chemicals in Williston's water supply.

ANSWERS AND EXEMPLARS

19: Climate Change, pages 104–105

Sample response: Phenell University's team had different results because of how they analyzed and adjusted the JMA data. Their statistical models filled in data from the Arctic and Anarctic, which are warming faster than the rest of the Earth. They also adjusted data from a 60-year period based on modern data collection techniques. Both of these adjustments led to a higher average temperature.

20: La Niña and Severe Weather, pages 106–107

Sample response: The prediction that there will be more hail events and tornado outbreaks in the Southern United States than long-term averages is correct as all three states in the South showed increases in severe weather.

The prediction that there will be fewer hail events and tornado outbreaks in the Midwestern United States than long-term averages is not correct as all three states showed increases in severe weather.